Emotional Literacy

The heart of classroom management

Dr Patricia Sherwood

First published 2008
by ACER Press, an imprint of
Australian Council *for* Educational Research Ltd
19 Prospect Hill Road, Camberwell
Victoria 3124, Australia

www.acerpress.com.au
sales@acer.edu.au

Edited by Susannah Burgess
Cover and text design by Divine Design
Typeset by Desktop Concepts Pty Ltd
Printed in Singapore

National Library of Australia Cataloguing-in-Publication data:

Author: Sherwood, Patricia.

Title: Emotional literacy: the heart of classroom management/Patricia Sherwood.

ISBN: 9780864318091 (pbk.).

Subjects: Early childhood education.
        Emotions in children.
        Emotions and cognition.

Dewey Number: 372.21

Disclaimer

All names of persons in this book have been changed and the case studies are unidentifiable
composites which represent themes children present in therapy rather than any identifiable
child's case.

To all children in the world whose heart stories have not been heard in their families or in the classroom and who weep silently or scream louder while they struggle to learn with their heads and master their bodies.

May their hearts, heads and bodies dance together in learning centres where the stories of the heart are honoured.

To all teachers everywhere whose hearts have longed to expand to find a space for the hearts of the children in their classroom and who know that feelings are the bread of children's lives.

May they be inspired with a way forward that is filled with hope, promise and possibilities for a rich feeling life in their classrooms.

To all parents who have struggled to find a space in schools and classrooms for their children's hearts to sing and flourish.

May they celebrate the coming of spring with a new language of emotional literacy and a new promise in educational settings.

CONTENTS

ACKNOWLEDGEMENTS

Special thanks to Tara Sherwood (aged 12), whose beautiful heart and colourful soul created the illustrations for this book. Her work gives colour and form to the voices of the hearts of children everywhere and has been my teacher in some of the many aspects of emotional literacy.

Thanks to Janet Ristic, whose wisdom from her years as teacher and deputy inspired me to write with passion and who assisted with the parent–teacher research project on classroom experiences.

Deepest gratitude to my teachers who have naturally promoted heart-centred classrooms with heart-created spaces, especially Teresa Daley and Sr Xavier.

ABOUT THE AUTHOR
AND THE ILLUSTRATOR

Dr Patricia Sherwood is a Director of Sophia College where she trains counsellors, teachers and human service workers in counselling and the non-verbal languages of emotional literacy. She is qualified in special education, counselling and psychotherapy and has a busy clinical practice in Western Australia and Queensland. She specialises in children, adolescents and relationship counselling. Dr Sherwood supervises over 15 free community counselling centres throughout Australia, staffed by the students and graduates of Sophia College, where children and adolescents are the most frequent clients.

Dr Sherwood is also a researcher at Edith Cowan University, and has lectured in the fields of psychology, social work, human services and education for over 30 years. She has developed a number of innovative training programs including a diploma and advanced diploma of holistic counselling, a graduate certificate in artistic therapies and a certificate in emotional literacy.

Tara Sherwood is fluent with the languages of emotional literacy, some of which she has taught her Mum. She plays the flute, composes her own music and plays in the school band. She loves to create songs and sings everyday. Tara loves nature, swimming in the dam with her labrador Sam, going to the beach and walking in the forest with Sam and her pet lamb. Since she was a small child, Tara has used colour and drawing to express her frustrations and joys. She knows how to get angry and how to move through it. Tara summarises school by saying: 'I need to learn how to solve problems, not how to fill in boxes'. Her ambition is to save the environment and contribute to world peace.

INTRODUCTION

Emotional Literacy is essential reading for parents, teachers and carers of children who have a deep commitment to the happiness of children and to educational processes that enliven children's hearts, minds and souls and which create holistic learning communities.

It is literacy for the whole child, not simply the child's mind. This is literacy for the feeling life, and it provides languages for the heart, which is at the centre of the wellbeing of each of us and especially our children.

Designed to turn classrooms into heart spaces, *Emotional Literacy* offers a range of non-verbal and specific artistic exercises that gives children the tools and languages to explore and manage their feelings. These exercises work because they are centred within a child's body and this overcomes the problem of the child knowing what the right behaviour is, but feeling unable to do it in challenging situations.

Children learn to identify the basic emotions of childhood: anger, fear, grief and loss, and aloneness in their bodies. They acquire tools to manage these emotions and to transform them into peace, safety, joy and connectedness with simple expressive exercises using sound, colour, movement, gesture, clay, sand and sensing.

The exercises are tailored for use with the individual child or for group activities. The model is designed to create an emotionally self-managing classroom in the long term. A place where the children identify their feelings and can move to a corner of the classroom designed specifically for them and where they can work through a particular feeling whether it is anger, grief and loss, fear or aloneness.

This book will be of interest to all teachers and parents who feel that they need fresh inspiration when working with the escalating problems of bullying, both from the experience of the child being bullied and the child doing the bullying. Here are body-based, non-verbal exercises that can make a difference to a child's experience very quickly.

Emotional Literacy promises a brighter future: for as children grow into adults they have tools to deal with their anger so that adult violence and abuse is minimised; they have processes for dealing with their grief and loss so that the incidence of depression may be reduced; they have tools to deal with their fear so that anxiety and stress in their adult lives may be minimised, and they have processes for reconnecting with meaning so that the despair arising from aloneness need not be their journey. We are on the verge of a Brave New World where those who flourish will be those who read their hearts' stories and use holistic processes to transform difficult and challenging emotions into courageous and flourishing lives. *Emotional Literacy: The heart of classroom management* lays the foundation stone for a healthy future for our children.

If we are to reach real peace … we shall have to begin with the children.

Mahatma Gandhi (cited in Larson & Micheels-Cyrus 1986)

CHAPTER 1

Hearts are at the centre

Cream Cake Charlie was the inspiration behind this book. He was five years old, in preschool and right 'out there' with his needs. His family history was rough—and tough—on Charlie, and he knew what it was like to spend nights in a domestic violence refuge. In fact, he considered it one of his homes. Charlie was a healthy lad with no attention deficit hyperactive disorder (ADHD), no Asperger's syndrome, no autism or anything else to which you could give a behavioural psychological label. However, Charlie was given to acts of violence against other children; hitting them and smashing their play things if he felt things weren't going his way in activities or games. Sometimes, the preschool teacher believed he could be violent for apparently no reason at all. When I met Charlie, the school psychologist had virtually given up on him. Initially she had had great success with Charlie because he loved cream cakes and would do a great deal to indulge in them. She had set up a behavioural management program in which every day that Charlie reached home time without hitting another child or destroying their play things, Charlie received a cream cake. This worked like magic for a few weeks, but gradually its effectiveness declined to the point that Charlie resumed his previous violent behaviours at about the same level prior to the intervention. Some people believed he was a bully, others said he was a victim of violence.

As Charlie swung his legs back and forward on the chair in my therapy room and smiled his wild freckled smile at me, he offered by way of explanation:

'You know I need to hit other kids more than I need cream cakes'. 'Where in the body do you feel that?' I asked Charlie, and he pointed to his heart. 'Let's step into your heart', I suggested to Charlie. Then, I asked him to use his x-ray vision and have a look around at what it was like inside his heart. Bravely, Charlie took a step forward into his heart, had a look around, and then stepped back out, with a sad and woeful look on his little face. 'It's broken', he said. 'Can you fix hearts of kids like me?' My heart at that moment held his heart and I said, 'Sure, we can fix hearts but it's keeping them safe from people who have forgotten about hearts that is the hard job'. And at that moment with tears in my eyes, I made a silent promise to Charlie and to all children in schools to speak up to create a space for heart-centred classroom management.

I could tell you much about what had broken Charlie's heart: grief, and loss of joy and safe playtimes; separation from his pets when he went to domestic violence refuges; fear his mother would be killed or injured badly by his dad; anger that he could not defend himself or his dog from his dad; resentment that his mum did not stop it and a feeling of emptiness. He drew this as great big black holes in his heart which desperately needed love, warmth, joy, friendship and peace to recover. I could tell you much of what I did as a therapist to restore and protect Charlie's heart and the changes in Charlie's life, but the gift from Charlie to me was awakening me to the need to create a process around resources for classroom teachers that enables them to manage the feeling life of children. It is not to suggest that teachers replace psychologists or therapists. Teachers have more than enough to do.

This is a pioneering book for developing multisensory processes to cultivate emotional literacy, a subject that has only come to our attention in the past decade. It offers skills for primary school teachers that include the following:

- A classroom management model for teachers that creates classroom spaces and enables the feeling life of children to breathe and flow towards healing, instead of being denied, repressed, discounted, or excluded from the classroom management process.
- An understanding of the non-verbal languages and skills needed to teach children to identify in their own bodies, hearts and minds the basic human feelings of anger, grief, aloneness, fear, judgement and the bullying and victim behaviours that arise from these feelings.

- A step-by-step group classroom process that uses the core emotions of children and mimimises the possibility that they will go on to develop major behavioural problems or psychological disturbances.
- Self-managing processes that are so simple and effective that even six-year-olds, once they have completed them in a group, can do by themselves. These self-managing processes can be done in a dedicated corner of the classroom as the children have been given the basic emotional literacy skills to identify and manage their core human emotions.

The time has come to incorporate emotional literacy into the school curriculum. It is not a new subject because feelings are at the heart of learning and living as a human being. It is simply a choice as to whether we consciously manage them effectively and teach children how to self-manage their feelings in an effective way using the languages of the feeling life, or, whether we ignore, repress or deny feeling and continue to focus on cognitive literacy alone. When feelings are addressed in schools, it is done using the verbal languages of cognitive literacy. These languages are inadequate for the task as evidenced by the increasing number of feelings that manifest into challenging behaviours that need psychological referral or psychiatric drug intervention in primary school children. If we introduce emotional literacy and use the languages of the feeling life, which are primarily non-verbal, to help children to identify and process their basic human feeling states, then many of today's school behavioural problems will not emerge.

One might ask why the feeling life of children is so important today. Children are always vulnerable to the emotional stressors of adults around them, but in the last few decades these have escalated. Divorce and marriage breakdown are reaching epidemic proportions with the associated grief and loss, fear, anger, aloneness, abandonment and resentment. The high mobility of families today means added grief and loss, and fear for children as they frequently move away from familiar surroundings, people and communities with which they have cherished connections. The number of prescriptions dispensed for medication for depression in Australia increased from 5.1 million in 1990 to 8.2 million in 1998. This rate of increase is the second highest in the world (McManus et al 2000). The World Health Organization (WHO) predicts that given the current trends, 20 per cent of all children will be depressed by 2020. This is of major concern given the tendency to treat children and adolescents with SSRI (selective serotonin reuptake inhibitors) drugs for depression rather than do in-depth profiles of family, lifestyle, nutrition and other stress factors and seek counselling interventions. A decade ago, it was noted that in the western world as many as one in every 33 children and approximately one in eight adolescents may have depression (Center for Mental Health Services cited in Psych Central 1996). It is disturbing that some current research is finding that youth on antidepressants are more likely to commit suicide than depressed youth who are not on antidepressants (Abbass 2006) or at least antidepressants make no difference to the level of suicide (Olfson et al 2003). Wright (2006) cites critical family traumas that trouble children and these include divorce, parental dispute, addiction, depression, unemployment, illness, crime, drugs, abuse by parents or being disowned or rejected by a parent. Furthermore, most of today's parents had no emotional literacy in their education, so despite their best intentions they are often panicked, troubled or flooded by their children's emotional life—a life they neither understand nor have the skills to help their child manage. Too often parents respond by denying or avoiding confronting feelings because it will also mean confronting their own limited skills to deal with emotions. Alternatively they may rush children off to counsellors, psychologists or psychiatrists for diagnosis. The fastest growth industry in mental health disorders for American psychiatry is children. Too often children are pathologised, labelled or drugged when all this could have been avoided by early intervention with parents, teachers and children employing basic emotional literacy skills.

In addition, there is a vacuum where there could be intrinsically meaningful and authentic ways of resourcing and meeting emotional needs. This vacuum has occurred because of the failure of modern society to provide sufficient core education in human values, which gives life meaning. This vacuum is largely filled by consumerism which requires us, for example, to eat more and more food even when we know this is killing us and encourages us to consume more and more goods and services even when we know this is destroying the planet. Consumerism is not the solution to deep felt aloneness, emptiness, anger, grief, abandonment, disconnection and despair. Increased violence in the streets, in homes, in schools and in the entertainment industry promotes fear and/or aggression in the psyche of children (Anderson & Bushman 2002).

Where are the images of beauty, truth, goodness, wholeness, warmth and love propounded by the Greek philosopher Plato in the mid fourth century BCE? Plato wrote about the essential components of healthy educational development of children. He argued strongly that one of the objects of education is to teach love of beauty and goodness. This touches the feeling life of children deeply. Steiner, the founder of Waldorf schools, would agree that the primary psycho-spiritual experience for the primary school child is to experience beauty while the primary psycho-spiritual task for the adolescent is to experience truth and authenticity (Lievegoed 1985). It is through their hearts that children live out life—the feeling life that is coloured by the sensory images of the natural world, peopled by the creative visualisations of their imaginations and warmed by their connection to the qualities that sustain life, hope, love, beauty, goodness and justice. Plato may be unfashionable, but the hunger in the human heart, especially of the primary school child for this 'bread' cannot be nourished with the stones of consumerism or the dominant ugly and often violent images of much electronic entertainment. Few children come to school physically malnourished in the affluent world, but many children come to school malnourished in their hearts. Teachers are left to feed the many hungry hearts of our children today and to master emotional literacy and they teach children the skills of identifying and processing their feelings, so that tomorrow their adolescent and adult lives may be lived more fully and more skilfully.

Experiences of the heart in the classroom: children, teachers and parents

How are the parents, teachers and children experiencing the feeling life of the classroom? To find out, a phenomenologically based survey of parents, teachers and primary school children in the south-west of Western Australia was conducted in 2007 by Sherwood and Ristic. This survey set out to obtain information on the experiences of the current management of emotions in the classroom. Interviewees were asked a series of questions as prompts for their reflections including:

- What are your positive and negative experiences of the classroom management of feelings?
- What changes would you like to see in the management of feelings in the classroom?
- How adequately do you experience current classroom management practices dealing with children's grief and loss, anger, fear and abandonment?

The questions were modified for the children into a language they could understand more clearly.

Children: Four core interpretative themes emerged from the children interviewed, which were as follows:

1 Children experienced that being punished for bad behaviour and getting rewards for good behaviour only worked for kids whose lives were pretty okay and who didn't have any big problems. As nine-year-old Temika explained: 'When kids are basically happy it is okay to send them to the office or stop them playing sport because they feel okay inside but when kids' hearts are broken that just makes them worse and they get angrier and angrier and sadder and sadder'.

2 Children experienced a need to help kids in classrooms to change bad feelings into good feelings instead of seeing them sent out of the classroom or to the principal's office. As eight-year-old Mimi said: 'Angry kids need to be calmed down. Get them to make a picture and make a special part of the room with calming down pictures and things to do so the kid can go and sit there and calm down'.

3 Children experienced many rules and lots of class work as being too hard for some kids and this was causing the kids to get angry or unhappy. As eight-year-old Marnie explained: 'Sad kids get sadder when they have to do work sheets. Then they get into trouble for being sad and not doing their work. Then they get detention and get put in the hallway and then they are really sad and angry too'.

4   Children experienced the need to do more physical activities with their bodies and imaginative activities with their hearts so they could feel happier at school. As 10-year-old Sam explains: 'I get into trouble for misbehaving sometimes because I am so sick of sitting down and doing worksheets when I want to run and I want to have some fun'. Eleven-year-old Tom also captures this feeling: 'I want to make buildings and do things that make my heart feel good, not more and more work sheets and writing and writing. It makes me tired and grumpy all of this writing all day. Then I get into trouble'.

Teachers: Seven core interpretative themes emerged from the teacher interviews, which were as follows:

1   Teachers experience their relationship with the child as the most important thing affecting the way the child expresses feelings and how difficult or easy it is to help the child with those feelings. As Ron explains: 'If a good relationship with a child is not a priority then no techniques will really work because relationship is the heart and soul of the classroom'.

2   Teachers experience the educational hierarchy as blocking or undermining teacher initiatives in the classroom to support children with their emotional life. Bob commented: 'The top down stuff is a real block to developing initiatives and supporting children to develop emotionally as well as cognitively … you are dictated to by accountability to the hierarchy'.

3   Teachers experience the need to help children with their feelings by supporting them to work through feelings and disagreements and build resilience. Ken commented: 'It's really important to teach kids to cooperate and get on with each other and build trust and safety. They need to learn how to get on with one another and not carry emotional baggage around.'

4   Teachers experience too much time consumed with documentation of teaching processes rather than actually teaching and supporting children with their emotions. As Ryan noted: 'The outcomes system is consuming the teacher's energy in filling in boxes instead of relationship building

with students and it is "dumbing down" education and making it difficult to give meaningful feedback to students or parents'.

5   Teachers experience the school psychologists as ineffective and poor communicators and listeners to teachers, parents and children. As Robin commented: 'The difficult problems are referred to the school psychologists who generally have poor listening skills and fail to reach the child or understand their feelings. The next thing is the child is suspended'.

6   Teachers experience the current behaviour management programs as 'bandaiding' rather than addressing emotional problems of a significant nature. As Meg explained: 'This behavioural management just doesn't work for most children with core emotional issues. Often children just can't cope, they don't all get aggressive. Some leave their bodies, just drift off into "la la land" so they don't have to face what's going on inside of their bodies, then they get labelled ADHD or something and someone wants to drug them ... it is all bandaiding when the real problem is their fear and the violence or abuse they confront daily at home'.

7   Teachers experience that children's family problems are being taken to school and become part of the classroom problems. As one teacher commented: 'It would be easier if children could leave their home baggage at the school gate when they come to school each day. If they could realise this is a different place with a different set of rules but they usually can't, and anger and sadness end up at school'.

8   Teachers feel inadequately trained to deal with children's emotions and constrained because it is officially not part of the curriculum. As Sarah states: 'To help children emotionally as a whole group you need skills and training and I don't feel I have them and it's not part of the curriculum which is all about filling their minds up. There is no room for teaching about feelings'.

Parents: Four core interpretative themes emerged which were, as follows:

1   Parents experience the school as too academically and task focused when their children need more free unstructured time and this pressure results

in the child feeling frustrated, angry and like a failure. Rena explained that her child had been happy in preschool but had become miserable in Year 1 because of the pressure on him to sit still and complete written tasks. He was isolated and alone up the front of the class whenever they had written tasks because he was a distraction. He feels bad about himself now and cries every morning when he has to go to school saying he is scared he can't do the work. The teacher seems unable to relate to his feelings.

2   Parents experience the school as failing to relate effectively to the individual needs of the child, which produces pressure on the child and feelings of inadequacy. Mary notes that her child is very dreamy and artistic and cannot finish routine worksheets and is often in trouble for dreaming. She feels that the school does not engage her feelings so she is not motivated to participate in learning, except in art activities which she completes with real enthusiasm and talent.

3   Parents experience the classroom as overly routine- and assessment-orientated, and believe that it does not adequately acknowledge the expressive feelings of their children. Susan complained: 'The pressure is always on to complete worksheets and make progress without checking the child's feelings. By eight years old my boy was suicidal. He just did not want to go to school because he was terrified of all the tests and the competitiveness of everything. He would say after school: "I just want to die if I have to do this everyday". It broke my heart and I went and told the teacher to lay off the work sheets; that I just wanted him to be happy and I did not care if he couldn't do cognitive stuff at the pace that she thought he should, and she said that she didn't think his feelings were important and that he would fall behind the rest of the class academically. I gave him lots of mental health days off school and he just survived the year. He completed his senior year at school and scored in the top handful of students in the state. There is a time for cognitive pressure on kids but it is not in primary school, there is enough of that in adolescence'.

4   Parents experience the school as inadequately meeting the needs of children in emotional pain through divorce, violence or abuse. Brin told

of the ongoing punishment of his son for aggressive behaviour in the school without the teacher understanding the boy's pain that his mother did not want him after the divorce. The teacher lacked ways of communicating with his son so his son could work through it instead of getting labelled as 'bad'.

This survey of the experiences of parents, teachers and children underscores the serious lack of focus on the feeling life of children in school and the inadequate strategies for dealing with everyday emotions of fear, anger, abandonment, grief and loss, and feelings of failure. There is an overemphasis on cognitive literacy at the expense of the child's emotional needs.

Heads, heads, heads on legs: the limits to cognitively focused learning and behavioural management

Let us briefly review why primary schools put so much emphasis on cognitive literacy and why emotional literacy has not been a focus in the classroom. The current dominant model in classroom learning is cognitive and it emerges from the work of Piaget who gave priority in his model of child development to cognitive learning (Petersen 1989). This means that children are pushed through cognitive stages of learning that are regarded as normative by Piaget, based on his sample of his two children in the 1900s who had a university professor father. Unfortunately, Piaget's developmental stages do not correlate with the development of many children, particularly boys, who are forced to read and write at six years of age. Biddulph (1995) makes the correlation between early failure at cognitive tasks and the development of bully behaviour in young boys at primary school and he emphasises that the school emotional environment for young boys is often intimidating and negative, which compounds problems. Piaget's preoccupation with cognitive literacy to the exclusion of emotional literacy has had serious consequences for the heart of the classroom. The Binet IQ test, which was supposed to measure intelligence, was purely focused on cognitive intelligence and any child that could not demonstrate the acquisition of cognitive skills had a high likelihood of developing low self-esteem or aggressive compensating behaviours to cover their feelings of rejection and failure.

It was only in 1983, that Gardner challenged the hegemony of the Piagetian cognitive model of classroom teaching with his model of multiple intelligences where he proposed that there are additional types of intelligence including linguistic, mathematical, spatial, intra personal (philosophical) kinaesthetic, musical (Kail & Cavanaugh 1996). We could add artistic, creative and interpersonal intelligences as well. At last, here was the opportunity to develop models of learning that integrate the sensory/feeling/thinking lives of children and which recognise emotional intelligence as one of the core intelligences in human beings. The Piagetian elevation of cognitive intelligence as the primary intelligence has unfortunately continued to intensify in school systems in the last two decades, despite Gardner's more inclusive model of intelligences. It appears that the scientific, materialistic, corporate world ethos promotes a cognitive model in education devoid of the feeling life, which is important to the development of ethics. It is a model without emotional literacy that limits our ability to deal with the devastating impact of industrialisation on the natural environment and ongoing wars and crusades against persons who are different in culture, ethnicity or values. The most critical intelligence lacking in today's fragile world is emotional intelligence, which requires emotional literacy to flourish just as cognitive intelligence requires cognitive literacy to flourish. Emotional intelligence underscores skilful human relationships and the ability to mediate difference, respect diversity, resolve conflict and recognise interconnectedness. The need for emotional literacy has never been higher as diverse human beings daily live more closely together on what is becoming the global village of planet Earth.

The neglect of emotional literacy in primary schools manifests in children as low self-esteem, resentment, bullying, fear, grief and anxiety, and, by adolescence, this emerges as depression, addiction, aggression, and self-harming behaviours such as cutting, anorexia, bulimia or refusal to attend school. Not only is the child's emotional life minimised or ignored in primary school because of an over-emphasis on cognitive development, but the behavioural management models dominating the primary school system in Australia are cognitive behaviourally based. While useful for the management of superficial behaviour issues, these models are unable to deal with the depth of the emotional feelings of children or adolescents. The forte of cognitive behavioural therapy (CBT) is behaviour management, but it is often ill equipped to deal with human emotional experience with its diversity, depth and individuality.

Too often CBT joins hands with the psychiatric drug management programs whose aim is to numb and repress further the feeling life to ensure that behaviours conform to the social norm. Research like Bernstein et al (2000) is typical of this approach where after clinical trials, they claim that imipramine plus cognitive behavioural therapy is more effective than placebo and CBT in improving school attendance and the symptoms of depression and anxiety in school-refusing adolescents. There is an increasing revolt among researchers on the selective reporting from studies sponsored by the pharmaceutical industry (Melander et al 2003). The drug industry profits from the prescription of drugs to youth for mental health issues so are not neutral sponsors of drug research. Abbass and Gardner (2004) argue in their survey that research that supports anti depressants in youth is six times more likely to be published and promoted than research that shows drugs to have negative effects. They propose brief counselling and psychotherapies for children and adolescents as an alternative as these treatments are cost-effective, do not have toxic side effects and increase the children's coping skills.

The best of cognitive behavioural therapy tends towards Glassner's (cited in Emmer et al 1986) model of intervention for dealing with problem behaviours in the classroom. Edwards (cited in Burden 2006) notes that the essential features include focusing on present behaviours; getting the student to accept responsibility and; assisting the student to develop a plan of change. Glassner argues that students are motivated primarily by consequences of their behaviours but there is strong experiential evidence to suggest otherwise and, in fact, children's relationships with the teacher and with each other engage their hearts and underlie the success or failure of such a model. As one eight-year-old primary school child so eloquently expressed it:

> We really love Mr B. (the principal) He plays sport with us at lunch time
> and makes us feel good when we see him. He likes us and likes visiting our

classroom. We like to do what makes him happy ... some of the naughty boys are good for him all the time ... because they like him and he likes us.

This story is so often evidenced in primary classrooms where the same cognitive behavioural management plans are in place throughout the school but some teachers succeed with even the most misbehaving child, without any difficulty. Most of these teachers do so because of the relationship of trust and respect they build with the child's heart. The child behaves well for them because they like the teacher and experience the teacher as liking them.

The focus of classrooms with hearts

The focus here is on giving teachers emotional literacy tools, skills and processes for working with primary school children to sustain children and classrooms with heart. Such classrooms have a language of emotional literacy that is largely non-verbal and an active feeling life that is palpable to children and teachers alike, and which enlivens and colours the fabric of the teaching and learning process. The task of restoring the heart of the classroom is complex and the following are the parameters which define and limit this work.

1   Reclaiming heart intelligence of children in classrooms

School systems in western cultures have focused around a psychology that splits the head from the heart. Vygotsky (cited in Daniels 2005) argued that psychology has been impaired by the separation of the intellectual from the motivational and emotional aspects of thinking and the supremacy given to the cognitive aspects of thinking. He proposed that it is impossible to remove all elements of emotion from thinking. Le Doux (1996 cited in Coles 1999) agreed, arguing that cognitive behaviouralism is a psychology that excludes a part of the mind; the critical part of the mind, the emotional life, leaving persons 'as souls on ice ... cold, lifeless creatures devoid of any desires, fear, sorrow, pains and pleasures'. In an effort to redress this inequity Goleman (1996) argued for the need to develop emotional intelligence as much as cognitive intelligence which he defined as knowing how to express one's emotions, manage one's moods, empathise with others, motivate oneself, and exercise interpersonal skills. Boler (1999) responded by critiquing the individualistic nature of this type of emotional life devoid of cultural contexts. So for example empathy would be expressed differently by Aboriginal and Torres Strait Islanders, Latin Americans, Anglo Saxons, and in different political contexts. Emotional intelligence is contextual and has different qualities some of which Goleman (1995) has identified. It originates not in the brain in the head but in the brain in the heart that has now been identified by Andrew Amour in his research on emotions (2007).

What is proposed here is a vibrational model of emotional life, preferably called the 'feeling life' which is based on McCraty et al's (2004) findings that heart intelligence is a vibrational phenomenon and hearts vibrate literally in response to energies up to two metres around them. This heart intelligence McCraty names 'intuition' and proposes that this is a sense that enables us to prepare for what is about to happen. The question in the classroom is whether we recognise or deny the experiences of heart intelligence or override its value by using a purely cognitive agenda. This book focuses on a way of integrating heart experiences into the cognitive learning processes so that neither is a poor or rejected relation of the other but rather head and heart are integrated, the heart infusing and softening the thinking processes and the thinking process lighting up the heart in a dance of mutual support within the body of the child.

2   Inclusive not special education

In education this division between cognitive and emotional intelligence has resulted in approving and rewarding children who manage to sublimate their emotions to the dominant paradigm and to label and pathologise children who do not sublimate their emotional life, even when these children are in terms of development physically or mentally within the normative cohort. Children who express grief and loss through self-harm or withdrawal; children who express frustration and or abuse through aggression or non-compliance; children who are rejected and abandoned and self-harm or act out, just to name a few categories of experience have been labelled as 'emotionally disturbed' and for several decades consigned to the special education classroom. However, grief and loss, anger, fear of rejection are core experiences in all human beings and become problematic only when denied, repressed, and ignored rather than acknowledged and transformed by processes that enlarge hope, joy, inner courage, peace and contentment.

This process of educating and empowering children to identify and change debilitating feelings into life-supportive feelings is 'emotional literacy'. It is for all children; it is not the province of special education. Certainly some children face many more difficult emotional experiences because of severe family system dysfunctions and they may need intensive counselling support outside of what can be provided in the class environment. However, if emotional literacy was taught in primary schools, the number of these children would diminish as they would have a language and be given tools to work with their emotions. If the classroom processes are enabling children to process their feeling life on a daily basis and supplementary counselling is available for children from challenging families, then the 'behaviourally disturbed' label may be largely dispensed with and classrooms can work inclusively. The focus of this book is on children who fall within the range of normal cognitive, and physical developmental patterns within their cohort. There is no attempt to assess its applicability to children with marked physical or cognitive developmental differences, or with children whose emotional development is within the spectrum of autistic behaviours. This is not to say that such applications within this book do not have relevance to such children but it is not within the scope of this work to address these children in the specific detail that is required.

3 Primary children not secondary

The focus is on primary school children and their classrooms because it is here the splitting of heads from heart intelligence really begins with a fervour that leaves children ill-equipped to deal with the emotional roller coasters of adolescence. The processes and tools offered in this book are tailored developmentally to the primary school classroom. In addition, studies of teacher satisfaction reveal that the primary school teacher's most important element of satisfaction is the relationship and affection for students (Nias 1989; Dinham & Scott 1997). In fact, many primary school teachers aim to create strong emotional bonds with their students (Hargreaves 2000) and this book supports a classroom process for developing emotional literacy and thus improving the quality of such a relationship.

4   Feeling life primarily of children not teachers

While the feeling life of the teacher is a critical part of the heart of the classroom and Chapter 9 will be devoted to this important subject, the primary focus of this book is on the feeling life of children in the classroom. Also, the feeling life of the teacher is very complex, encompassing the feeling qualities of the effective teacher, the emotional attachments and projections of teachers, impacts of authoritarian hierarchies, high stress curriculum outcome processes and excessive and debilitating bureaucratic demands (Hargreaves 2000). It demands a book in its own right. Here, the focus is on the feeling life of the teacher in relationships with children in the classroom in the context of creating and maintaining a classroom with heart through the teaching of emotional literacy.

5   Classroom not the organisational constraints

Finally, one of the profound impacts on the ability of teachers to create and process the feeling life of primary students is the neglect of the feeling life of primary school children by the educational policy and administration bureaucracies that set agendas for schools. These agendas are focused upon cognitive literacy as though it were the only valuable literacy and are increasingly rationalised, and cognitively driven with behavioural measures like targets, outcomes, performances, competencies, and skills. This rationalist paradigm for policy development echoes the sterility of the economic rationalist agenda currently dominating society. While production of economic goods and services increases, the quality declines and we have an epidemic of mental health issues arising from the frustrated, oppressed and ignored feeling life of people. This rationalist organisational framework limits the teacher's ability to create a classroom in which emotional literacy can be cultivated. The rationalist framework dominating educational policy-making today needs to be challenged at a macro level. However, bureaucratic reform is not the focus of this book even though its constricting effect on teachers and students is acknowledged. Rather, this book focuses on what we can do to revive the heart of the classroom.

It assumes that while we could wait for the bureaucratic policy-making structures to change and humanise, we can act now at the micro classroom level and speed up the process of change by planting the seeds of the trees we wish to see flourish—the seeds of emotional literacy.

Creating a heart-centred learning environment

The time has come to create a flourishing heart of the classroom as teachers of primary school children. Much has already been done by primary teachers to create feeling relationships with their students, and to work towards using learning processes that engage the feeling life such as in the arts with movement, dance, colour, clay, music, drama, physical activity, yoga, and sensory connections through the heart with nature. We need to recognise and celebrate these triumphs in what is a generally unsupportive bureaucratic organisational climate.

This book plants another seed towards creating the flowering of the heart of the classroom by providing educators with a model of classroom practice which integrates the day-to-day feeling life of children as whole human beings and focuses on the human conditions of anger and frustration, grief and loss, rejection and abandonment, loneliness and emptiness. These are the states of the ordinary day-to-day mind of human beings. This story is about how they can be turned into flowers of emotional literacy in the garden of the classroom.

References

Abbass, A 2006, 'Merits of psychotherapies' (letter), *Canadian Medical Association Journal*, vol. 175, no. 1. Accessed 31 January 2008 at www. cmaj.ca/cgi/content/full/175/1/61-a

Abbass, A & Gardner, D 2004, 'Informed decision making with depressed patients: Medications and psychotherapy options', *American Family Physician*, vol. 69, no. 9, pp. 2071–2, 2074.

Anderson, CA & Bushman, BJ 2002, 'Pyschology: The effects of media violence on society', *Science*, vol. 295, no. 5564, pp. 2377–79.

Bernstein, GA, Borchardt, CM, Perwien, AR, Crosby, RO, Kushner, MG, Thuras, PO & Last, CG 2000, 'Imipramine plus cognitive-behavioural therapy in the treatment of school refusal', *Journal of the American Academy of Child and Adolescent Psychiatry*, vol. 39, no. 3, pp. 276–83.

Biddulph, S 1995, *Manhood: An action plan for changing men's lives*, Finch Publishing, Lane Cove, NSW.

Boler, M 1999, *Feeling power: Emotions and education*, Routledge, New York.

Burden, P 2006, *Classroom management: Creating a successful K–12 learning community*, 3rd edn, Wiley & Sons Inc., Hoboken, NJ.

Coles, G 1999, 'Literacy, emotions and the brain: An invited contribution'. Accessed 31 January 2008 at www.readingonline.org/critical/coles.html

Daniels, H 2005, *An introduction to Vygotsky*, Routledge, New York.

Dinham, S & Scott, C 1997, *The teacher 2000 project: A study of teacher satisfaction, motivation and health*, University of Western Sydney, Penrith, NSW.

Emmer, ET, Evertson, CM & Worsham, ME 2006, *Classroom management for middle and high school teachers*, 7th edn, Prentice Hall, Boston, MA.

Gardner, H 1983, *Frames of mind: The theory of multiple intelligences*, Basic Books, New York.

Goleman, D 1996, *Emotional intelligence: Why it can matter more than IQ*, Bantam Books, New York.

Hargreaves, A 2000, 'Mixed emotions: Teachers' perceptions of their interactions with students', *Teaching and Teacher Education*, vol. 16, no. 8, pp. 811–26.

Kail, R & Cavanaugh, J 1996, *Human development*, Brooks/Cole, Pacific Grove, CA.

Larson, J & Micheels-Cyrus, M (eds) 1986, *Seeds of peace: A catalogue of quotations*, New Society Publishers, Gabriola Island, BC.

Lievegoed, B 1985, *Phases of childhood: Growing in body, soul and spirit*, Anthroposophic Press, Hudson, NY.

McCraty, R, Atkinson, M & Bradley, TR 2004, 'Electrophysiological evidence of intuition: Part 1 The surprising role of the heart', *Journal of Alternative and Complementary Medicine*, vol. 10, no. 1, pp. 133–43.

McManus, P, Mant, A, Mitchell, PB, Montgomery, WS, Marley, J & Auland, ME 2000, 'Recent trends in the use of antidepressant drugs in Australia, 1990–1998', *Medical Journal of Australia*, vol. 173, no. 9, pp. 458–61.

Melander, H, Ahlqvist-Rastad, J, Meijer, G & Beermann, B 2003, 'Evidence b(i)ased medicine—selective reporting from studies sponsored by pharmaceutical industry: Review of studies in new drug applications', *British Medical Journal*, vol. 326, pp. 1171–3.

Nias, J 1989, *Primary teachers talking: A study of teaching as work*, Routledge, London.

Olfson, M, Shaffer, D, Marcus, SC & Greenberg, T 2003, 'Relationship between antidepressant medication treatment and suicide in adolescents', *Archives of General Psychiatry*, vol. 60, no. 10, pp. 978–982.

Petersen, C 1989, *Looking forward through the life span: Developmental psychology*, 2nd edn, Prentice Hall, Sydney.

Plato 1955, *The Republic*, trans. HPD Lee, Penguin, London.

Psych Central 1996, 'Childhood depression'. Accessed 22 May 2007 at www.psychcentral.com/disorders/depressionchild.htm

Sherwood, P & Ristic, J 2007, *The experience of emotional management in the classroom*. Unpublished manuscript.

Thanks for the memories 2007, television program, ABC Television, Sydney, 12 April.

Wright, D 2006, *Classroom karma: Positive teaching, positive behaviour, positive learning*, David Fulton Publishers, London.

… her heart lived in no cherished secrets of its own, but in feelings which it longed to share with all the world.

George Eliot (1860)

CHAPTER 2

Feelings: opening the heart

What is the heart? The heart is not just a pump ensuring through its systolic and diastolic motion that there is a continuous flow of lifeblood to our body. The heart is the most exquisitely sensitive and intelligent organ in the human constitution. Recent research by McCraty et al (2004a; 2004b) indicates that the heart has an electromagnetic field of two metres which it projects around us. It can sense feelings and react to them even before they become visible. So for example, research subjects, when shown pictures of emotionally evoking images while their brain and heart were wired to monitors, reported responses that showed that the heart preceded the brain in responses on all occasions. In addition, the heart would respond with the appropriate feeling even before the emotionally evoking image appeared on the screen. When six-year-old Billie says: 'Miss, he hurt me. He looked at me', Billie's heart is speaking the truth of the experience of anger or hostility or rejection that it is sensing. He is not to be dismissed as overly sensitive. We need to think of thoughts and feelings as having an energetic reality. What we think actually affects ourselves and other persons and the heart is a very sensitive antenna of other people's thoughts and feelings towards us. It is critical to understand this because children's hearts are particularly vulnerable and exposed to the powerful thoughts and emotions of adults. Their hearts respond to the thoughts and feelings of adults that ultimately determine their self-esteem, confidence, motivation and desire to live rather than die. Further documentation on the extraordinary capacity of the heart completed by McCraty and Childe (2003) in their monograph *The Appreciative Heart* demonstrates that the heart has 'intelligence', 'a brain' and 'a memory'. In some indigenous cultures such as the Australian Aboriginal, and Kalahari Bushmen when asked where they think, they point to their hearts. It is incomprehensible to them that anyone could think only with their heads. In fact it has become evident that high order thinking that is insightful, skilful and focused depends upon a rhythmical and synchronised relationship with the heart's beat. Arguelles et al (2003) propose that in holistic education, the heart's rhythms must be addressed first. If these rhythms are chaotic or disordered, which occurs when people are under emotional stress, then higher cognitive functions of clear thinking, memory, reasoning and retention of knowledge are limited. To maximise our human potential brain, heart and body literally have to be 'in sync', that is, their energetic patterns need to be interrelated in a rhythmical and patterned way.

The heart as the seat of life's rhythm

The heart gives us the gift of rhythm in our physical bodies with the regularity of heartbeat and supports the rhythmic movement of the lungs in our breathing processes. In the anthroposophic medical model, the heart and lungs are seen as the critical organs that connect the outer sensory world with the inner life of a person and hence are regarded as the home of the soul, that is, the source of experiential life derived from our interaction with the sensory world (Bryant 2006). It is interesting that the contemporary revival of interest in the feeling life in classrooms is termed 'soul education' and is beautifully expounded by Rachael Kessler (2000) in what has become the foundation work on the subject in classrooms. She talks about the seven gateways to the feeling life for establishing connection, character and compassion in the classroom. These include joy, creativity, silence, initiation, transcendence, connection, meaning and purpose.

Feelings monitor our moment-by-moment relationship to our external environment and act as the flags of our quality of experience. When our feeling life is healthy, we are breathing fully and there is a flow of breath naturally occurring through our bodies as the heart and lungs work their rhythmic dance in the body. It is at these moments that we feel the harmony that comes from the movement of the natural life rhythms. We feel relaxed, fully human and at these moments are capable of our best and most fulfilled performances. At the deepest level this is our heart's gift to our lives and it is through this rhythmic flow that children are best able to express their feeling life. Anger and fear are emotional states that are the result of loss of rhythm in the breathing, which displaces the heart from the centre, and leaves either the cold and hardened mind or instinctive bodily responses to take over. When this occurs, there is no active feeling life or empathy for another child and it is here, in this vacuum, that bullying, cruelty, and meanness are born.

When the breathing is restored and the heart can be re-seated at the centre of the human life then we are capable of the best of human feelings: love, wonder, awe, joy, compassion and empathy as we experience connectedness within ourselves and with each other. When the heart is not at the centre of a child's life then the intellect or thinking life becomes dry and desiccated. Life becomes routine, the colour is drained away and our children become numbed, stressed or daydream to escape this aridity. Godwin (2001) cites Hillman's description of the heart–mind separation as 'thought (that has) lost its heart'. We could go further and say that when the heart is not at the centre then the willing life, located in the lower part of the body produces actions that are in danger of becoming exploitative, competitive or destructive to self, others and the environment. Here, deeds lose their heart. Bryant (2006) argues that morality and values are seated in the heart and a culture or society that ignores the heart is destined for instinctual survival processes that can rapidly deteriorate into greed and a destructive compulsiveness to control others.

Hearts are at the centre: balancing the upper and lower poles

Hearts are the centre of the child, and hence of classroom management. If we see the child as a thinking, feeling, and willing being and locate these activities primarily in relation to head, heart and limbs, we immediately recognise the importance of the feeling life centred metaphorically and literally in the centre of the body (Lievegoed 1985). The heart is located in the centre of the body mediating the life rhythms between the head and the limbs, the thinking and feeling life. Bryant (2006) describes this graphically:

> The physiological trinity of head, trunk, and limbs is evident in the neural-sensory dominance of the head, the respiratory emphasis of the middle body, and the metabolic-limb character of the lower body. Obviously, the central location of the rhythmic system is the key to its role as mediator: Psychologically, the head is the reflector of sensing and thinking: the heart and lungs reflect feeling and emotion; the limbs and metabolic organs reflect will and action.

The heart is at the centre and essential for the balance. In anthroposophical and eastern systems of medicine and health, the human being is seen as having seven energy centres or chakras with the heart being the central energy centre. Daver (2004) describes these in detail in the yogic system of health derived from Hinduism and Buddhism. The three lower centres are the survival chakra (red at base of the spine), the sexual or creative chakra (orange), and the solar plexus or chakra at the navel (yellow) which comprise the lower pole of the human energetic system. The upper three chakras are the throat or truth speaking chakra (blue), the forehead or chakra of insight (purple) and the pineal chakra on the crown of the head (violet), which comprise the upper pole of the human being's energetic system. The upper and lower poles intersect through the heart chakra (green) which governs the feelings. Balance between the lower pole which is related to the lowest three chakras and controls willing, and the upper pole which is related to the highest three chakras and controls thinking can only be achieved when the central chakra, the heart chakra is fully functioning. Then the feeling life mediates willing and thinking, that is, body, heart and mind to produce a healthy functioning human being (Evans & Rodger, 2000). The flow of this energetic balance between thinking, willing and feeling, that is, mind, body and heart is represented diagrammatically by Sherwood (2007), opposite.

As a consequence of emotional trauma restricting the breathing, habitual patterns of imbalance in the flow of breath and energy lead to two main

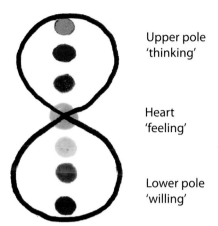

Upper pole
'thinking'

Heart
'feeling'

Lower pole
'willing'

Figure 2.1 The balanced whole person.

profiles of imbalance. In both patterns the feeling life is constricted and not functioning well and this in turn causes imbalances in the mind and body. In upper pole imbalance, thinking dominates and in lower pole imbalance willing dominates. In both models the feeling life is crippled, constricted and is crushed. These models of imbalance between the upper and lower poles are documented further in Bott (1995). This model of upper and lower pole imbalance in relation to thinking, feeling and willing is central to the model of a human being which influences education in Steiner schools and medical practices in anthroposophically-based hospitals.

1 Upper polarity over-development

This is illustrated diagrammatically below and occurs when the upper pole is over-developed at the expense of the lower pole. As a consequence overemphasis is on the head activities of thinking. Here there is a tendency to ungrounded activities, poor interpersonal boundaries and to an overactive preoccupation with thoughts and ideas and an over-sensitivity to other persons.

These types of children are often creative, imaginative, and have no difficulty assessing spiritual or non-material experiences. Often they live in expansive worlds of ideas, and score highly on indices relating to creativity, imagination and thinking. However, these children are not grounded and can lack the will to manifest ideas as deeds. This results in difficulties dealing

Figure 2.2 Upper pole over-development— overemphasis on thinking

with the challenges of life, with confronting situations and with managing physical and, later in their lives, financial issues. These children have poor boundaries and can be victims of bullying and as adults the doormats or energetic garbage bins for other people because of their oversensitivity to the world around them. The feeling life is not contained but rather bursts upward. They often feel as though they are victims and experience feelings of being vulnerable and unsafe. Physically they are prone to illnesses relating to the lower limbs, the reproductive system and the metabolic system. These children need to engage in gardening, looking after pets, physical exercise and activities that involve movement of the lower limbs of the body, which engage the passions or feeling life. Above all, these children need to learn boundaries and to say 'no' or to 'speak up' for themselves and their needs. Musical instruments that favour the lower tones such as drums and didgeridoos are good for these types of children.

2 Lower pole over-development

This profile is illustrated below where the will dominates the thinking and the feeling life is constricted.

Such children can be very successful in the physical world particularly in arenas relating to sport, power and acquisition of material things. In their

Figure 2.3 Lower pole over-development

excesses, they are prone to greed, control and power at the expense of human and environmental relationships. This is the classic profile of the 'bully' who wants to have it his or her way in the material world. It is difficult for them to access feelings, imaginative ideas or spiritual and artistic experiences. They lack sensitivity in human relationships as the heart centre is restricted and often have over-developed boundaries, experiencing others as 'road bumps on the path to getting what they want'. They need to develop their feeling life and the imaginative creative sides by taking up some artistic activity, playing a musical instrument such as the violin, or flute, working for the poor or needy in a voluntary capacity, or helping at animal refuges. All these things can help restore the feeling and imaginative life and evoke empathy which is a difficult feeling to access regularly for these children.

The institute of Heart Math in the USA has coined the term 'physiological coherence' to describe the ideal state of human functioning which maximises our potential as human beings in learning situations. Here the heart's rhythms form the foundation and when they are ordered and not stressed by negative emotional states of fear, anger, hatred or grief, then they harmonise both the brain and nervous system activity to produce our most insightful and error-free activities (McCraty & Childe 2003).

Opening the heart: creating a safe and trusting space in the classroom

This involves attention to four core aspects: the relationships (both between peers and with the teacher), the classroom space, the feeling processes in the classroom, and the non-verbal languages of the feeling life.

1   Relationships: the heart of the classroom

Relationships are the essence of the feeling life and they determine the nature of the heart space of a classroom, for they are the centre of the classroom 'atmosphere'. This includes relationships between children, and relationships between the teacher and students, and principal and students. Relationships are based on feelings and these cannot be feigned because the heart readily detects feelings as McCraty, Atkinson and Bradley (2004a) demonstrate in their research on the electrophysiological evidence of intuition. To illustrate, two children aged 10 and 11 visited school with their mother who was thinking of enrolling the children there. The school principal showed the parents and the children around the grounds, smiling and saying hello to the children they passed in the school yard. In the car on the way home the children commented: 'He is a phoney. He did not really mean the nice things he said to the children. It was just part of what he thinks he should do and say. Really he is not interested in kids'. There are many guides for teachers on how to speak to children that explore how to phrase the conversation and which words to use. Carl Rogers' (1978) work on empathetic languaging is inspiring. However, essentially the heart responds to the vibrational or non-verbal level of the message and primary school children are very focused on their hearts. Even when they don't understand words, they interpret through the non-verbal messages they receive. They are not deluded by teachers who 'say the right thing' but do not have integrity with their own feelings. Hence, in terms of the basic gesture of heart that a teacher needs to promote to create an alive and genuine feeling life in the classroom is akin to Carl Rogers' (1978) core qualities of the counsellor, namely: unconditional positive regard, authenticity and empathy (Ivey, Ivey & Simek-Morgan 1993). Research on what works in counselling or in core human relationship has validated these qualities.

Unconditional positive regard: This is the most challenging of all the qualities of the feeling life but essentially it means that children need to feel liked for who they are, and not judged as bad, no good, stupid, and unreliable. Typical comments of children in classrooms experiencing this are: 'she treats us all the same and she likes all of us', 'even when we get told off for stuff we've done, we know he still likes us'. Children who complain of 'teacher's pets', 'boys being bad' or tell me that 'Josef is no good' do not live in a classroom of unconditional positive regard. Unconditional positive regard is a room in which behaviours can be labelled as skilful or unskilful, but the person remains separate and does not become the label of their behaviour. By persistently holding an attitude of positive regard towards children and teaching them to hold this attitude towards each other, the classroom becomes a safe space for the vulnerable heart and all its feelings. Let us take the example of Joe who had a tough front to the world. He was 12 years old and told his classmate, Mary, who was crying because her mum was very ill, not to be so 'stupid'. The teacher and class members told Joe that the comment was a judgement and needed to be cancelled because it hurt Mary's feelings. Joe apologised to Mary. A few weeks later, Joe broke down in class because his mother had been taken to hospital the night before after his father had violently attacked her. He slouched on his desk and tears rolled down his face. No one judged him and Josie came and touched his hand and said: 'I know it must be pretty hard for you'. Often people need in-depth personal work or counselling to break through the block to their hearts, but sometimes just the example of another person showing unconditional positive regard for them is sufficient to open their heart.

Authenticity: Essentially authenticity is being honest about who you are and having integrity. Again, children pick this up non-verbally through their heart's energy field because they experience incongruence between what the teacher says and who they are or what they do. Mark, a 12-year-old described his experience of this to me: 'Mr Brown keeps telling us to respect others, not to call them names or make jokes about them but that is exactly what he does to us in class and he can't take his own treatment because if we make jokes about him or call him names, he immediately punishes us. I don't think it is fair'. As teachers, we need to show the qualities we ask of our students and when we fail we need to be able to acknowledge failure and reaffirm our commitment to becoming the quality we support. The story is told of a mother who took her young son to Gandhi. She wanted Gandhi to tell her son not to eat sugar, as it was doing her son harm. When she arrived Gandhi replied: 'Please come back next week'. The mother was puzzled, but brought her son back the next week. Gandhi told the young boy, 'It is not good for you', and then joked with the young boy. When the mother asked Gandhi why he could not have given her son that advice the preceding week he replied: 'Last week I too was eating sugar' (Easwaran 1997). Teachers are not perfect and children are very forgiving but open honest dialogue needs to occur when the teacher fails to model the standards they are setting for the students. Authenticity is critical for the safe and supportive heart space.

Empathy: An Aboriginal man best described empathy to me as 'when someone walks beside you and offers help if you need it. It's the opposite of standing above you and crying over your head'. Empathy occurs when the heart feels understood and this can be achieved by a heartfelt presence, a look, a gesture, an affirming gesture of support. Empathy is essential to understand the needs of others and to gain a broad perspective on everyone's needs and interests in a conflicting situation. It is that part of us that seeks a win–win situation respecting our own needs while being mindful of another's needs. Hart and Hodson (2004) in their beautiful work *The Compassionate*

Classroom identify empathy as one of the core languages of the classroom which is heart centred.

2 The classroom space

To create a heart-centred classroom space, it is essential to remember the rhythmical nature of the heart and create a setting that has predictability and rhythm in time and activities, so that children experience it as a harmonising experience. Throughout this book, a range of activities or processes will be presented that teachers can use daily to assist students to remain in their heart rhythms rather than acting out or withdrawing during classes. As previously noted, research by Arguelles et al (2003) emphasises that if the heart's rhythms are disrupted then cognitive learning processes cannot be maximised. These classroom processes will focus on the core feeling issues of anger, grief and loss, fear, emptiness and abandonment, empathy and its absence (bullying), and speaking up. A chapter is dedicated to each.

In addition though, particular children will have specific additional needs to nurture their hearts at different times during the day. This means that certain parts of the classroom need to be allocated to core feelings so that when a child is flooded by a particular debilitating or disruptive feeling of either anger, grief, aloneness/abandonment or emptiness, they have a dedicated space to move to—a space with known predictable routines that they can use to transform the feeling back to a sense of wellbeing and harmony. This means that the feeling life is given space to continue breathing during the class day, even when other activities are being undertaken that have other feelings attached to them or are largely cognitive. Much disruptive or day-dreaming behaviour in classrooms occurs because feelings of anger, fear, loss, grief, aloneness, abandonment and emptiness surface during the class activities or are brought to the classroom from home or other environments and the child is so flooded by them they have difficulty continuing with the set class routines or activities. The teacher has neither the resources nor the time to take each child through their feelings at unique moments and times so a process for self-transforming these feelings needs to be taught and available for the child to access. This is a core component of the language of emotional literacy in the classroom.

It is suggested that each corner of the primary classroom be dedicated to one core aspect of the feeling life. Children can move themselves to the space and take responsibility for changing certain key feeling states that are otherwise disruptive to their continuous learning. The corners for the key feelings are diagrammatically represented below:

Sand play Unhcard story	*Clay* Anger defusing
Water colour Grief and loss	*Colour/sound resourcing* Emptiness/aloneness

Each of the following chapters will be dedicated to these core feeling states and specific directions for establishing each corner and the processes to be undertaken therein will be detailed.

3   The feeling processes in the classroom

These will be explicated in the chapters relevant to the particular core emotions.

4   The non-verbal languages of the classroom

Our first language is not English, rather it is the non-verbal language of the feeling life namely: sensing, sounding, gesturing/ moving, visualising, and breathing. These remain the ways in which our primary experience of the world is created and communicated within ourselves and to others. These non-verbal languages are the primary languages of emotional literacy. They must be integrated with verbal language in the teaching of emotional literacy, if we are to keep the heart of the classroom pulsing with healthy life force.

Sensing: an energetic language—expressing and transforming experience

Sensing refers to the human ability to sense the flow of energy within and around us. We sense danger around the corner; we have an uneasy feeling near a particular person which is later confirmed by an unpleasant experience. We sense our fear, delight, pain and pleasure, long before we have translated our feelings into words. We sense the knot in our stomach, the lump in the throat, the bad feeling in the stomach. Rather than ignore or repress these important bodily experiences, we need to educate our children to read them. The ability to sense is critical in connecting to our own experience and to other beings (human, animal, plant) and to the creation of empathy, the core connecting human feeling. Cultures which are rooted in natural environments such as Australian Aboriginal culture have highly developed sensing for deriving information from the natural worlds which is essential for their productive survival. Virtual reality, however, is virtually soulless and relegates our feeling life to the passive rather than an active initiator and interpreter of our life experiences. Children need to be reminded of the first core language of emotional literacy, namely sensing. Sensing also helps increase their safety in the world as it is one core language in sensing an abuser or bully coming towards them and enables them to get out of the way. The protective behaviours program uses the language of sensing to teach children to sense into their bodies if someone is coming towards them or is near them who gives them a 'scared or yucky feeling' in their bodies. It alerts them to move quickly away from them and towards a safe person or place. Reminding children of this language and how to use it would immediately reduce some cases of bullying, as the victim, through sensing, recognises the early warning signs and takes action to move to safety. Details of this program can be viewed at: www.protectivebehaviours.com.

Breathing: an energetic language—expressing and transforming experience

We need to teach children how to uncover why they stop breathing fully into parts of their body as this is the key to their emotional numbness and disconnectedness (Brazier 1997). Children need to notice they have contracted their breath and then stop, and understand why. What is the pain that is difficult? They need to name the feeling and re-connect bodily sensing with feelings. Then thinking has a chance of being insightful and skilful rather than reactive. Through class activities such as yoga, meditation and the range of active physical sports, children can learn ways to restore the flow of the breath through their bodies. There is remarkable improvement in the behaviour of children who have been outdoors and run around for 10 minutes to restore the rhythmic flow of the breath. In all subjects, children need to notice when they are not breathing fully and stop, rather than push through with a task without a support process for reconnection with their feelings, with self and others. Angry, grumpy, violent children, have first restricted their breathing within themselves and caused disruption in the heart rhythms before they transfer their disrupted emotional states onto other children. The breath being invisible is difficult for children to grasp but a medium is provided through gesture. Gesture is frozen breath. Gesture and movement enable children to view exactly what is going on inside them. This is another of the core languages that needs to be revived in emotional literacy. McCraty et al (1999) have developed a raft of skills programs to restore the heart rhythms in middle school children and provide the foundation that results in improved cognitive skills. Such programs are trade named as 'Heart lock-in' and 'Test=edge'.

Movement/gesture: an energetic language—expressing and transforming experience

There is a considerable body of research on gesture, more popularly known as body language. Pease (1992) is one of the most popular. Gestures are the primary map of the thinking/feeling life. Pease (1992) cites the research of Mehrabian (1971) which found that the total impact in communication is 7 per cent words, 38 per cent intonation and inflexions and 55 per cent non-verbal gestures and movements. Tagar (1999) elaborating earlier work by Steiner (1921) proposed that every human experience can be directly expressed in a gesture by every functioning person and be universally understood. Steiner (1921) developed an elaborate system of movement called curative eurythmy to be used in the resolution of childhood developmental problems that affect learning.

In most subjects, gesture and movement can be incorporated and should not be restricted to drama alone. When a child is speaking in an unskilful way, ask the child to freeze into the gesture of how they are speaking and notice the shape of their body. How do they feel when their body is in this shape? How are they likely to relate to others when their body is in this shape? How could they change the shape of the bodily gesture? Ask a second child who has been put down to freeze and gesture how they feel, so the first child has the opportunity to gain concrete insight into the impact of their thoughts and actions on another person's feelings. Gesturing and moving is the ideal way to enliven learning processes for it engages all the non-verbal languages of sensing, breathing, visualising, and sounding. It is a method of bodily learning that uses acting, creativity, imagination, insight and movement to connect with the individual's own body and feelings and to connect with other's feelings.

Modern spontaneous free dance and movement integrate body, mind and feelings and the body movement enables one to express and transform inner emotions. The research on dance and movement in transforming a range of difficult physical and mental behaviours is impressive. One example is the work of Koshland, Wilson and Wittaker (2004) who found dance interventions effective in reducing aggressive behaviours among 54 multicultural elementary school children who undertook the program. Goldberg (2006) notes the importance of dance in learning a range of subjects including science, biology and social science. Through gesture and dance children can express feelings that otherwise remain repressed and which may surface inappropriately through aggression. The Tiwi indigenous peoples communicated to each other and resolved many of their differences through dance and movement. It is a powerful medium for the expression of the feelings.

Sound: an energetic language—expressing and transforming experience

As early as 1921 in *The Alphabet* (1982) Steiner propounded the importance of the sounds of human speech. He defined his holistic theory of sound experience, claiming that the dynamics of the sounds of speech provide the whole structure of the human constitution. Vowels express the inner experience of persons, while consonants are the way in which the personal relationship to the outer world is expressed. Steiner in *Speech and Drama* (1924) proposes that every aspect of human experience can find its counterpart in a sound pattern and that mostly the sounds of human speech are capable of representing in their many different combinations, the entire human experience.

Tagar (1994) graphically describes how waves of human experience create sounds:

> ... human experience ebbs and flows, swirls and pulsates within its own echo chambers. There also live the echoes of the human's own creative world: the echoes of one's own thoughts and feelings, imagination, responses and deeds. Events of inner life alongside events of outer life take place and pass away with the ongoing flow of time. But their echoes remain, continuing to resound: below time, above time, not in time at all. Within the chamber of the subtle bodies of human being, bodies which are made entirely of resonances, the echoes of experience never cease to resound ... In these patterns of resounding, live all the aspects of experience one has ever had. From there they govern the basic patterns of one's life ...

In essence, every experience has a vibrational pattern which lodges within the emotional life and sinks down into the physical body. Tagar (1994) noted how vowels and consonant sounds can be used to represent a range of emotional experiences, and to quickly move through experiences so these experiences do not become recurrent problems, such as recurrent bouts of anger. For example, when a child is angry, then the breath is restricted. If the child can sense the anger in their body, then with a loud 'g' (gh ... gh ... gh), repeated three to five times they can release and restore the free flow of breath. This is much more skilful than releasing the anger by acting out, hurting others or imploding within oneself and creating illness and bitterness. Similarly, there are sounds that can be used for resourcing, for bringing missing qualities of love and connectedness back into the child's life following experiences of grief and loss or abandonment such as 'l', 'm', and 'n'. There are sounds that can be used to keep the child's space clear of bullies such as 'd' or 'b'. All sounds have a character that lives and moves in our bodies and the character of the sound creates and sustains, clears or builds particular emotional and physical states (Tagar 2000). All teachers need to familiarise themselves with the healing and transforming power of each particular sound in the alphabet. These are particularly important for helping children honour their grief and loss, their sadness, their anger, their aloneness and for helping children to have simple tools to resource themselves. Children often know this instinctively and will sing or hum to themselves during the day if this is not repressed by adults around them.

Visualising/colour: an energetic language expressing and transforming experience

Visualising is the firstborn of the imagination, the faculty of the feeling life whose companions are intuition and inspiration. It is through visualising that we can create new possibilities, new futures. In the marvellous story of Harry Potter, rich with the fruits of the imagination, Hermione and Harry are horrified to witness Hagriff's friendly monster Buck Beak being executed for responding to the taunting Malfroy. But Professor Dumbledore unveils the secret power of the imagination to recreate the scenario so that on this occasion they visualise themselves rescuing Buck Beak and taking him to a safe place.

Quantum physics and body–mind research is now demonstrating that this is not just a child's fantasy but the thoughts that we create and visualise release chemicals that travel down to the receptors in the cell walls and this increases, over time, the number of receptors for anger, or love or hatred, depending upon what we visualise and think. Visualising is a powerful language and we need to alert children to its power and to teach them that thoughts and feelings are realities, just of a different vibration to buildings, chairs or physical bodies. Through visualising, the imagination of children is harnessed to problem solving, to healing their hearts and reconnecting to themselves. Encouraging the expression of the imagination in every act of schooling—art, science, reading, maths, environmental studies— is critical to maintain contact with the feeling life. In learning, there should be a grand doorway for the engagement of creative and imaginative capacities if we are to cultivate emotional literacy in the classroom (Deasey 2002).

Conclusion

In essence, we work to enlarge the space for the heart centre in the classroom so that the excesses of cold and detached thinking alone can be softened by the sensitivity to the feelings of ourselves and others. Perhaps then we can contribute to creating an education process where ethics flourish—because ethics arise from the good heart permeating the thinking processes with warmth and light and sensitivity to others. The active feeling life will also temper the brutalising impact of willing alone, which otherwise results in cruel and tyrannical acts. It is the good heart that leads the will to deeds that are compassionate and caring rather than exploitative and abusive. We strive to create a classroom in which feeling experience is the weft, and cognitive activities the warp of the fabric of the classroom atmosphere. Cognitive literacy and emotional literacy must go hand in hand to produce a healthy flourishing human being. The heart rhythms remain the foundation which profoundly influences the rhythms of the mind and the body. If the heart life is content and calm, then the thinking will be insightful, focused and productive, and the body, healthy.

References

Arguelles, L, McCraty, R & Rees, R 2003, 'The heart in holistic education', *Encounter: Education for meaning and social justice,* vol. 16, no. 3, pp. 14–21.

Bott, V 1995, *Spiritual science and the art of healing: Rudolf Steiner's anthroposophical medicine,* Healing Arts Press, Rochester, VT.

Brazier, D 1997, *The feeling Buddha: A Buddhist psychology of character, adversity and passion,* Robinson, London.

Bryant, W 2006, *A journey through time: Biographical rhythms,* Rudolf Steiner College Press, Fair Oaks, CA.

Daver, HS 2004, *My true reality: A guide for inner awareness through meditation,* Daver, Sydney.

Deasey, RJ (ed.) 2002, *Critical links: Learning in the arts and student academic and social development,* Arts Education Partnership, Washington, DC.

Easwaran, E 1997, *Gandhi, the man: The story of his transformation,* Nilgiri Press, Tomales, CA.

Eliot, G 1860, *Adam Bede,* Harper & Brothers, Publishers, New York.

Evans, M & Rodger, I 2000, *Complete healing: Regaining your health through anthroposophical medicine,* Anthroposophical Press, Great Barrington, MA.

Godwin, G 2001, *Heart: A personal journey through its myths and meanings*, William Morrow, New York.

Goldberg, M 2006, *Integrating the arts: An approach to teaching and learning in multicultural and multilingual settings*, 3rd edn, Pearson Education, Boston, MA.

Hart, S & Hodson, VK 2004, *The compassionate classroom: Relationship based teaching and learning*, PuddleDancer Press, Encintas, CA.

Ivey, AE, Ivey MB & Simek-Morgan, L 1993, *Counselling and psychotherapy: A multicultural perspective*, 3rd edn, Allyn and Bacon, Boston, MA.

Kessler, R 2000, *The soul of education: Helping students find connection, compassion and character at school*, The Association for Supervision and Curriculum Development, Alexandria, VA.

Koshland, L, Wilson, J & Wittaker, B 2004, 'Peace through dance/movement: Evaluating a violence prevention program', *American Journal of Dance Therapy*, vol. 26, no. 2, pp. 69–90.

Lievegoed, B 1985, *Phases of childhood: Growing in body, soul and spirit*, Anthroposophic Press, Hudson, NY.

McCraty, R, Atkinson, M, Tomasino, J, Goelitz, J & Mayrovitz, H 1999, 'The impact of an emotional self-management skills course on psychosocial functioning and autonomic recovery to stress in middle school children', *Integrative Physiological and Behavioural Science*, vol. 34, no. 4, pp. 246–8.

McCraty, R & Childe, D 2003, *The appreciative heart: The psychophysiology of positive emotions and optimal functioning*, The HeartMath Institute, Boulder Creek, CA.

McCraty, R, Atkinson, M & Bradley, RT 2004a, 'Electrophysiological evidence of intuition: Part 1. The surprising role of the heart', *Journal of Alternative and Complementary Medicine*, vol. 10, no. 1, pp. 133–43.

McCraty, R, Atkinson, M & Bradley, RT 2004b, 'Electrophysiological evidence of intuition: Part 2. A system-wide process?', *Journal of Alternative and Complementary Medicine*, vol. 10, no. 2, pp. 325–36.

Pease, A 1992, *Body language: How to read others' thoughts by their gestures*, Camel Publishing Company, Avalon Beach, NSW.

Rogers, C 1978, *Carl Rogers on personal power: Inner strength and its revolutionary impact*, Constable, London.

Sherwood, P 2007, *Holistic counselling: A new vision for mental health*, Sophia Publications, Brunswick, WA.

Steiner, R 1921, *Eurythmy as visible speech*, trans. V & J Compton-Burnett, Rudolf Steiner Press, London.

Steiner, R 1924, *Speech and drama*, Rudolf Steiner Press, London.

Steiner, R 1982, *The alphabet. An expression of the mystery of man*, Mercury Press, Spring Valley, NY.

Tagar, Y 1994, 'Awakening to the inner resounding of human experience with philophonetics counselling' in Y Tagar 1999, *Philophonetics: Love of sounds*, Persephone College, Melbourne.

Tagar, Y 1999, 'Stress management: The use of non-verbal expression in stress management' in I Gawler (ed.) *Medicine of the Mind conference proceedings*, The Gawler Foundation, Melbourne, pp. 246–66.

Tagar, Y 2000, 'Participatory therapy: The non-verbal communication and the healing team of client, therapist and the life-body' in M Cohen (ed.) *Pathways of Holistic Health conference proceedings*, Monash Institute of Public Health, Monash University, Clayton, Vic, pp. 163–82.

The angry people are those people
who are most afraid.

Dr Robert Anthony (Cook 2007)

CHAPTER 3

Anger: taming the tiger

Tiger Tim was 12 when he came to see me in therapy. There had been an incident in the school playground where he had terrified some children, threatened a teacher with a stick, and the school had called in the police. It all began when Tiger Tim was not selected for a lunchtime footy team. It was important to be in a footy team because all the boys loved to play footy and the boys engaged in it so seriously one would have thought they were playing for sheep stations. This day, one of the other boys, Joe, who delighted in teasing other children, mocked Tiger Tim with 'see, nobody wants you'. Tiger Tim turned into a wild tiger and grabbed Joe by the neck and began to strangle him. The teacher on yard duty tried to intervene. By this stage, Tiger Tim was in the grip of a black rage and grabbed a loose fence post and went for the teacher who beat a hasty retreat. It took a couple of police to corner him and remove the stake because Tiger Tim was a speedy runner.

Some people believed Tiger Tim was just uncontrollable and should be suspended indefinitely, others said he was very dangerous, others prophesied that he would end up in the juvenile justice system, definitely before he was 15. I wondered what he was so afraid of that his rage was so great. I have noticed with children that fear and rage are connected: the greater the rage, the greater the fear lying just underneath it all. I liked Tiger Tim because he had a great sense of humour and laughed a good laugh when the candle on the wall above my head melted and droplets of wax streaked my hair purple.

When I asked him, what he wanted to change in his life, he said he wanted to go back to school because he has some friends there he missed. 'Tim,' I said, 'do you know what made you so wild with Joe?' He looked at me blankly, then sort of guessed, 'He's mean to me'. 'But how does that make you feel?' I asked. 'Bad,' he groaned. 'And where in your body do you feel the bad,' I quizzed. 'In my heart,' he said. 'Well if you want to go back to school, we better take a journey to the bottom of your heart and do some repairs,' I suggested, 'So how about you take a step forward and imagine you are stepping into your heart. Then grab the anger in your heart with both hands and throw it out on the wall with a big loud 'gggraahh' and see how it splats on the wall, so we can see the face of this monster'.

Tiger Tim was a smart young man and in a matter of seconds he had completed what I asked him to do. 'Make the shape of your anger as it hits the wall in clay,' I requested. He made a magnificent big flat splat of clay with broken pieces coming off it from all directions and radiating from the centre of the splat. It was big and ugly and taking over the space. 'Okay,' I said, 'let's find what is underneath that big splat of a monster. Step back into your heart to just before you got really angry and grabbed Joe and tell me how you feel trapped. Do you feel like you are under a big rock, trapped between two pieces of concrete, trapped in a twisting device?' Tiger Tim tentatively stepped back into his heart and replied: 'I feel like I am trapped in the middle of a big block of concrete and I can't move or breathe. It is suffocating me'. Then Tiger Tim made the shape of the place in which he was trapped and it was right in the middle of a big cube of clay which he sculptured with real care and precision.

I could see that Tiger Tim had a talent for making things by the way he worked the clay into just the most precise cube-like shape. 'Now Tim,' I directed, 'step back into this cube in your heart so that your whole body fits in the cube'. Tiger Tim stepped into the middle of the cube and instantly curled up into a tiny ball on the ground; his arms were around his legs which were pulled up to his chest. 'Hey, what are you feeling in there?' I asked. 'I'm really scared because my Mum has just died and I don't know what is going to happen to me. Maybe I will just die because no one will want me'. My heart held Tiger Tim's little heart and the fear was palpable and I knew I was looking into the face of our greatest fear: the black hole of abandonment and aloneness. I was aware from his case notes that mum had died of a drug overdose when he was only five years old. Tim never had a father or at least never had a father that he had known. It was true no one had wanted him. A distant relative volunteered to take his sister because she did not have a girl but he was placed into foster care. The first family returned him after six months because circumstances changed and they moved overseas. The second foster family decided to give up fostering after he had been with them for two years and he returned back to a state home where the children were cared for by paid staff. He was now in his third foster home.

Belongingness is the second basic need on Maslow's hierarchy, and it was very clear to me that Tiger Tim had had very little. The wound in Tiger Tim's heart was a gaping sore of being rejected and abandoned. No wonder he went to terror when Joe teased him about being rejected for the football team. This was Tiger Tim's Achilles heel. He made in clay the little curled up one inside the cube in clay. Together we looked at this sad little foetal figure. 'What do you think about him, Tim?' I asked, and he replied 'He is very frightened'. Tim rocked back and forward as he looked at this sad abandoned little clay boy who we found at the bottom of his anger, then asked: 'What do we do with him?' We'll have to help recover his happiness I replied, we just can't leave him in your heart any longer.

So began the journey of helping Tiger Tim work to heal the six-year-old abandoned Tim. It involved 10 sessions which were essentially designed to bring back all the qualities that were missing into the five-year-old's life by resourcing him with sound, colour, gesture, and by using clay and paints to create a new energy around this five-year-old. Of course, Tiger Tim had to do boundaries as well and learn how to protect his heart and how to speak up without anger. We also joined 'aunties and uncles', a support network for children and found a mentor for Tim who made him feel special and loved and made special time for Tim on a weekly basis. Tim had never had this sort of attention before in his life or this sort of fun. It brought the gold in his heart to the surface and the light back into his eyes. Tim did not end up in juvenile justice. He obtained an apprenticeship at 15 years of age through his mentor who was a painter and has not looked back. I passed him in the street one day and he smiled his great smile and I knew his heart was mending.

Anger in the classroom: imploded or exploded

Today, the single greatest emotion expressed at school that challenges teachers is anger. Anger is a multi-coloured creature that begins with the subtle hues of frustration, irritation and/or resentment before manifesting as full blown black rage which is exploded as anger. Anger can also be imploded, particularly among females, in some cultures, for example, some Asian cultures, and introverts. Here the anger is not expressed outwardly but turned in upon the self and then expressed through secondary behaviours such as criticism, bitchiness, gossip, and mean and revengeful acts that range from sticking sharpened pencils into other students to damaging their possessions. Imploded anger is endemic when an individual feels powerless in the face of a situation or person that they experience as powerful and capable of punishing them, whether emotionally or physically. Such anger in the classroom arises in children who are being abused in the family system, or when children feel frustrated in the school system that is not meeting their needs and where they feel afraid or unable to speak up. In imploded anger the expression of the anger is removed from the trigger incident and is acted out later on in a different situation. In contrast, in exploded anger, the person reacts immediately to the trigger by shouting, hitting, smashing or verbally berating another person. This is much easier to identify because the person's reaction is immediate to the trigger and is a more common expression of anger among boys, within European and South American cultures, extroverts and persons with a choleric temperament. These two main expressions of anger can be summarised opposite using the analogy of red and white elephants developed by Tagar (Sherwood 2007). In the chart opposite, the major differences between imploded 'white elephant's' and exploded 'red elephant's' expressions of anger are summarised.

Imploded anger 'white elephants'	Exploded anger 'red elephants'
Turned inwards to self	Turned outwards to others
Trigger incident not observable	Trigger incident observable
Ridicule, name calling, meanness, gossip, bitchiness	Physical or verbal violence
Contributes to illnesses like stomach ulcers, stomach aches, arthritis	Contributes to illnesses like strokes, high blood pressure, heart attacks
Fears punishment if anger expressed	Uses anger to intimidate others

Table 3.1

Anger and speaking up: languages in the classroom

Anger has a number of red flags that can be identified in the verbal language that is used in the classroom. It is a language which is characterised by criticising, blaming others, using 'you' terms and telling others what they think and feel. 'You make me feel bad,' 'you make me mad', 'you don't do what I want'. It also has a number of observable body languages such as constricted breathing, gestures that are off balance such as arms or hands or legs reaching out past an individual's personal space and not returning to the individual's centre, and that dull often glazed look in the eyes or a burning black look in the eyes in moments of intense anger or rage. The anger response is also out of proportion to the trigger incident. An example is six-year-old Sarah, who is told she must take her library reading book back to the library and grabs onto the book, and screams and kicks on the ground when the teacher tries to enforce the directive. Also in anger, children will often triangulate other children into an alliance against the persons with whom they feel the anger or engage in behaviours such as name calling, gossip, and ridicule. Many of these characteristics of anger language are akin to Hart and Hodson's (2004) 'jackal' language identified in their inspirational book

The Compassionate Classroom. They propose a contrasting 'giraffe' language which is the language of giving and receiving. It has much akin to what is described as the language of Speaking Up (Sherwood 2007). In speaking up, the person speaks from the position of the insightful self, owning their experiences: 'I feel angry when you scribble on my drawing because I really like that picture and I wanted to give it to my mother for her birthday and I need you to remove the scribbles'. They state their experience, name what they need, speak directly to the person and the emotional tone is in proportion to the trigger. In addition, the body language shows a continued flow of breath, a bright, alert and present look in the eyes and centred body gestures that remain and return to the personal space of the speaker. The contrast between the reactive languages of anger and the speaking up languages of healthy classroom communication are summarised in the table below:

Anger: reacting to others	Speaking up: for needs
Constricted breathing: feels tension in the body	Flowing breath: does not feel tension in the body
Not owning experience 'you make me feel', **'jackal language'**	Owning experience 'I feel' **'giraffe language'**
Dull glazed look in eyes or burning black look in moments of rage	Bright, alert present look
Judgements/blaming/criticising others **'jackal language'**	Non-judgemental/ accepting others experiences **'giraffe language'**
Gestures off centre of body	Centred body gestures
Unaware of needs **'jackal language'**	Stating needs clearly **'giraffe language'**
Response out of proportion to the trigger event	Response in proportion to the trigger event
Triangulate other parties into alliances against the trigger person **'jackal language'**	Speak directly to the person involved **'giraffe language'**

Table 3.2

Models of managing anger in the classroom: the good, the bad and the ugly

The dominating contemporary classroom management models are based on cognitive behaviourism that generally focuses upon non-conforming behaviours and develops a series of consequences for these behaviours. This may start with one cross on the board, then a second cross on the board, then a third cross on the board and then more punitive consequences such as exclusion from the classroom, forced attendance in another classroom or time outside the classroom or in the principal's office. This model of behaviour management does not address the deeper needs of the child and intensifies the separation between mind and heart. It is derived from cognitive rather than emotional literacy paradigms. As Fien (2003) notes it 'enshrines personal empowerment through rational critical reflection: ignoring other forms of knowledge and experience, particularly heart knowledge and experience'. While this model may work for children whose hearts are basically emotionally whole, for children whose hearts are battered, such strategies for managing anger fail dismally. This model is too simplistic, too primitive, to address the complex dynamics of the heart and the feeling life that underlies expressions of anger. It is a model focused on producing behavioural outcomes for the short term, rather than watering the tree of the needs within the child's heart. It often claims successes which are really repetitive failed attempts to find the roots of the child's needs and address them. Take the case of Martha.

Martha was undergoing a behaviour modification program because she was aggressively pushing and shoving other children in the classroom on a regular basis. Her academic performance and motivation to learn was also very poor. She was placed on a token system and after four sessions with the school psychologist using a cognitive behavioural model, stopped her behaviour. The school psychologist claimed a success. However, about one month later, Martha, began to steal attractive drawing equipment from children in the classroom and even the teacher. She was sent back to the school psychologist who again introduced another token system and claimed a further success, when Martha stopped that behaviour. However, within a month or two Martha began to disrupt games in the classroom by violently throwing over the board games, often in the middle of a game. So the story goes, routine trips back to the school psychologist with the aggressive behaviour simply changing from one form to another. The worst scenario is that this level of intervention continues; fails to address the deeper causes in the feelings, and by 14 years of age Martha is suspended indefinitely from school for throwing a chair at a teacher; the chair then went through a window. The long-term neglect of the heart, the real needs of the feeling life, becomes ugly in adolescence when the capacity to express anger escalates. Furthermore, as Goleman (1996) emphasised, it is the emotions that determine the individual's achievements in life so if you are emotionally distressed it impacts directly on other areas of achievement in life.

Teachers and principals are realising that this cognitive model alone is no longer adequate to deal with anger in the school environments. Something is missing. Hart and Hodson (2004) in *The compassionate classroom* draw attention to the feeling life of children and the need for a return to patterns of classroom communication that are respectful, sensitive and address the deeper needs of children to give and receive. They present a range of verbal communication strategies that work to diffuse anger at its roots. This work is typical of the peace education programs that focus on win–win goals of meeting each other's needs and having an emotionally positive classroom. It is a program that creates a learning community based on giving and receiving, and listening with empathy, rather than a classroom of hierarchical power, based on fear and guilt, which is low on empathy and which uses emotionally depleting strategies of judgement, blame, criticism, shame and guilt.

Hart and Hodson's work articulates effectively the verbal dimension of change required in the hearts and minds of children to prevent anger arising and how to manage it when it does arise. However, it does not address the body heart mind connection expressed through the non-verbal languages which are the core of emotional literacy education and which the activities of this book focus on. It does not provide sufficient understanding or strategies for Tommy who, despite all the right verbal strategies, still finds himself in uncontrollable explosive anger, or Mark who despite naming what are his needs, feels driven to stick his sharpened pencil into Bob who sits next to him. Many children can internalise positive processes for communication of needs but at the critical moment fail to do so and collapse into anger. Josie, aged nine, explained the struggle to me:

> Well I know how to say what I need and how to ask what the other person needs and not to say 'You, you' or blame someone else but sometimes I can't do it. Like I just get so mad when I don't win the game and before I can stop I'm yelling or tipping the board over. My body seems to take over and I'm left watching it. I can't get it to do what, in my head, I know it should do. It's like I know I should not eat too many lollies because then I get worms and I hate that. Mum says I have a choice not to eat too many lollies but I don't always feel like I have a choice. Sometimes my taste buds just take over and I just eat too many lollies. It's not me doing it, it's my tastebuds.

Essentially, we need to go further than re-connecting the head and the heart. We need to reconnect the body, heart and head together because the three are required to act in unison, if we are to be truly effective teachers of emotional literacy. The following strategies are typical of emotional literacy processes for managing anger in the classroom and are based on the integration of body, heart and mind. They begin by calming and ordering the rhythms of the heart by restoring the breath. The first step in emotional literacy is to be able to name and identify a feeling that you experience in your body. A feeling is not in the head, it is expressed in the body through the contractions in the flow of breath.

Body-based holistic classroom interventions for managing anger

Group exercise 1:
learning to read the signs of anger arising in the body

We need to understand the flow of the breath because this is the easiest way to predict when a child is heading towards anger. It is also so simple that children can learn to predict in their own bodies when they are heading towards anger and defuse it before it erupts with an explosion or an implosion. The basic understanding is that for emotional wellbeing and the most skilful emotional responses, the breath needs to flow freely through the body down to the tips of the toes. It flows rhythmically in a dance governed by the heart and the lungs.

Step 1   Children stand up and practise breathing down to their toes.

Step 2   Children breathe down to the tips of their toes repeatedly until they imagine the breath coming out of the tips of their toes.

Step 3   Children then think of what they are angry about and watch where in the body the tense angry feeling lives. (When anger is beginning to build up, we contract the flow of breath and the part of the body in which the breath is contracted will be experienced as tense, uneasy, constricted or shaky.)

Step 4   Children place their hand on the part of their body where the tension feels strongest. Literally, this tension squeezes the breath out of parts of the body, and as we leave the body so does our capacity for insight; the highest part of us that directs, through the will, our ability to make skilful decisions and control unskilful emotions like anger.

Step 5   Children draw this tension. Is it a knot, a black lump? Is it like a ball of string? Alternatively, they could make the shape of the lump in clay. Or they may draw the sort of animal that this tension represents: Is it a grumpy bear? A lion?

Step 6   Help children understand that this is the early warning sign of beginning to get angry.

Once the above exercise is completed and understood then follow on immediately with Group exercise 2.

Group exercise 2:
defusing bodily anger and restoring the heart's rhythm

Children need to learn as a group in the classroom to defuse anger and other strong feelings so that class outbursts do not need to occur. This exercise can also be conducted with the whole class whenever the teacher feels the energy of the class is out of rhythm, tense or prickly.

Step 1   Ask the children to stand up and close their eyes and breathe down to their toes. Make sure no one is facing anyone else's back. It is ideal if they can all face the wall.

Step 2   Ask them to place their hand on the part of their body that feels uncomfortable, tense, bad or yucky.

Step 3   Suggest they collect the tense or yucky feeling into a ball with their hands and throw it away against the wall. As they throw it away say loudly 'g' (gh ... gh ... gh ...).

Step 4   Ask the children to take a step backwards and shake off the yucky/angry feeling by shaking both their hands.

Step 5   Repeat Steps 2–4, three to five times until the children are making clear sounds of 'g' against the wall. Usually this is sufficient to remove the 'uncomfortable' feeling from their bodies.

This very simple body-based exercise, first developed by Tagar (1996), will reintegrate body, heart and mind and the children will return to an insightful, calm position of their natural emotional and bodily rhythms. The 'g' is a very important consonant because it literally unblocks the blocked breath and children should learn how to do clear 'g's (gh ... gh ... gh ...) that bounce off the wall. Children that have the most difficulty producing clear, crisp 'g', are those who suffer from imploded anger and it is important they receive extra coaching to learn to articulate a clear 'g' that bounces off the wall. They can practise by hitting a ball against a wall with a tennis racquet, and each time it hits the wall repeating 'g' very crisply. Children cannot speak up for themselves or their needs when 'g' is stuck in their throat. The consonant vowel, 'g', repeated clearly and projected at least two metres ahead with the voice, is not only excellent for defusing the bodily feeling of anger but for defusing tension in the body.

Just as we shower daily to remove physical dirt, so we should 'g' daily to remove emotional tension stored in the body. It only takes one minute and it is a great investment in a child's daily mental health wellbeing. It is recommended the whole class do 'g's at least once a day at an established time in the day, so it becomes an automatic skill to defuse tension and create a space for speaking up in a heart-centred classroom. Children feel the benefit of 'g' in their rhythmic systems and will soon remind you, the teacher, that it needs to be done.

Bill was a young seven-year-old in therapy for fighting other children in the school playground with uncontrollable outbursts of anger who learnt to do 'g'. Every day he practised 'g' and it was the first thing he did when entering the counselling room. He lived in an abusive family system on his access weekends, so there was a build-up of anger on a weekly basis. On this particular day, I was doing a court assessment and had replaced his regular counsellor. I started the session by having him complete a sand tray. After about two minutes he stopped and looked intently at me then spoke up: ' Are you a real counsellor or are you just a pretend?' I replied: 'Why do you say that Bill?' He replied: 'Because real counsellors know about anger and the first thing you should always do at the beginning of a session is do your 'g's and get rid of your anger'. 'You are right, Bill', I said. 'I forgot. Let's do our 'g's now'. Bill's aggressive outbursts at school greatly reduced over the time of therapy and Bill continued to do his 'g's every day to sustain the change.

As follow-up, when you notice a child's breath contracting in their body with the energy of beginning anger, the way of drawing it to the child's attention is to ask: 'where in the body do you feel anger?'

Group exercise 3:
breaking through blocked speaking

The compassionate classroom model relies heavily on children speaking up for their needs but this is not easy for many children who have grown up in environments where speaking up for your needs is punished. The following exercise in clay can be completed by all class members so they learn a tool for eliminating the blocks to speaking up for their needs when these blocks occur. This process is suitable for all age groups and is documented in length in Sherwood's *The Healing Art of Clay Therapy* (2004).

Exercise: To remove the block to speaking up for your needs

Materials

- Working size board usually about half a metre by half a metre. Tables covered with sheets of plastic replace the need for individual boards.
- An airtight bucket of standard pottery clay in one of the earth hues. The clay usually retails for around $14 per 20 kg and this quantity is suitable for up to 15 children.
- Towel and access to water for cleaning hands.
- Three good hand-sized balls of clay per child.

Step 1: to express the shape of the block

Ask the child to recall a time in which they did not speak up for their needs. Concretise the details of the situation as much as possible by asking them to recall the person they need to speak up to and what they need to say.

Then ask them to find the part of the body that feels most uncomfortable when they recall the incident. Proceed by directing the children to:

- Step into that part of the body and sense how the breath/energy is not moving or stuck in that part of the body. Is it like a ball of rock, a ball of string, a twisted rope, a hole or something else?
- Exit or step backwards then gesture the shape of the block.
- Make the block in clay.

Step 2: to make a tool to break through the block

- Ask the child to imagine what tool would be needed to break through the block.
- Give an example, such as if the block is made out of wood you might need an axe or a saw. If it is made out of metal you might need a blow torch etc.
- Have the child make the tool to break through the block in clay.

Step 3: breaking through the block

- Ask the child to apply the tool to the block using a sound and gesture of the tool.
- Get the child to repeat the sound and gesture of the tool until the child experiences that the block has been broken through.
- Have the child make in clay the shape of the block that has been broken through.

> **Step 4: speaking up**
> - Ask the child to speak up to the person or situation. Ask the child to speak out loud or write it down on paper.
> - Have the child repeat this process until the child senses the power of speaking up.

Example of blocked speaking

Ben was nine years old and could not speak up and tell Tom not to open his school bag and take his toy soldiers away to play with other children. This was making Ben angry.

Step 1: the block

Ben experienced discomfort in the throat. When he stepped forward imagining he was stepping into his throat Ben experienced a big lump of coal in his throat which he made in clay.

Step 2: the implement

Ben made a big hammer out of clay which he said was needed to smash down the block using the sound 'b.b.b'

Step 3: breaking through the block

Ben then applied the hammer to the block with a loud 'b.b' until it was all broken. He was then asked to step back into his throat and make the shape of what was inside his throat now. He said it was clear and the lump had gone and he made a big ring in clay saying that was his empty throat.

Step 4: speaking out

We then practised speaking up for his need and he said: 'I feel angry when you go through my school bag and take my things out. They belong to me and I need you to ask me if it is okay first to take my things and play with them from my bag'.

Exercises for individuals in the anger expression corner of the classroom

Once the class is familiar with the holistic body, heart and mind processes outlined above for managing anger and speaking up, then it is time to unveil the anger corner of the classroom. This corner needs a good curtaining off from the rest of the room with absorbent materials on the wall so that when the student throws off the rising anger with loud 'g's against the wall, the sound is absorbed. In this corner, also place a container of clay and a clay board, so that a child may take themselves through the speaking up sequence outlined above, and they can actually name their needs.

In emotional literacy, we are aiming to develop in children skills to read their bodies and hearts and to act in a self managing way to address their feelings. Children need these skills in the classroom, but they also need these skills for life. My experience is that children given the skills and the opportunities are very accurate in their identification of their feelings and managing them. Jim, a six-year-old boy whose parents were separated and who was forced to have access to his mother even though her partner was sexually abusing him, was very angry that he had to go to his mother every weekend. Jim was taught how to throw his anger away using 'g's and Jim did this every Monday on returning home from access. His fighting with other children at school diminished once Jim started downloading his anger with 'g's every week. It is a shame and morally unacceptable that Jim was the victim of a legal decision that was destructive to his wellbeing, but at least Jim had tools to download his anger rather than allow it to run over into his school life and destroy his friendships with his peers. The anger corner is great, because it provides a legitimate place to download anger that a child can feel arising in his or her body, so that it is not displaced and misplaced through expressions of hostility towards children around them.

As children become familiar with the process of identifying anger arising in their bodies and in other children's bodies, they can help each other by reminding each other: 'Hey, you feel like you're getting angry now. Do you want to go to the anger corner?' Also, because children can use their whole body and breathing system to download their anger, they return to the group breathing more fully and more centred and balanced in their actions. Because the heart rhythms have been restored they are then able to be present to learning tasks as well.

Conclusion

Remember that anger is a flag that the child's breathing has become contracted and that there is tension in the child's body, and disruption in the rhythmical flows of the feeling life of the heart. It is calling attention to the primary need to restore the rhythmical flow of the breath. The child learns to throw the tension away with a series of loud 'g's, which is a quick, efficient way to restore the flow of body, heart and mind. The child who is breathing into their body is able to use 'giraffe' talk and speak up for their needs without having to resort to aggressive behaviours to signal the tension within. Learning to defuse anger is a skill that becomes a gift each child can bring to create a heart-centred classroom, and a happier family life. It is a gift that continues to multiply blessings into their adult life, as they know how to identify the emergence of anger and to exit anger. This skill will not only result in their own adult mental happiness but reduce domestic violence, interpersonal conflict and parenting conflicts. Conquering anger is the foundation for peace within ourselves, in our families, in our communities and in the world. Children long for world peace. As teachers we can teach children that the first and most powerful step towards world peace is conquering our anger and creating peace within.

'Let there be peace on earth and let it begin with me.'

References

Cook, J 2007, *The book of positive quotations*, 2nd edn, Fairview Press, Minneapolis.

Fien, J 2003, *Learning to care: Education and compassion*, Professional lecture at Griffith University EcoCentre, May 15. Accessed 5 February 2008 at www.griffith.edu.au/ins/collections/proflects/fien03.pdf

Goleman, D 1996, *Emotional intelligence: Why it can matter more than IQ*, Bantam Books, New York.

Hart, S & Hodson, VK 2004, *The compassionate classroom: Relationship based teaching and learning*, PuddleDancer Press, Encintas, CA.

Sherwood, P 2004, *The healing art of clay therapy*, ACER Press, Melbourne.

Sherwood, P 2007, *Holistic counselling: A new vision for mental health*, Sophia Publications, Brunswick, WA.

Tagar, Y 1996, *Philophonetics: Love of sounds*, Persephone College, Melbourne.

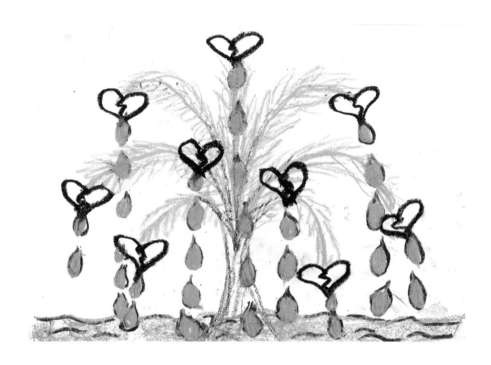

Sorrow concealed, like an oven stopp'd,
Doth burn the heart to cinders …

William Shakespeare, Titus Andronicus

CHAPTER 4

Grief: climbing the weeping willow

Melancholic Mary was eight years old when her mother brought her to counselling because she had failed all her Year 3 subjects. Her mother was bewildered because Mary had been dux of Years 1 and 2. She was a bright child and the school psychologist said her IQ was 135 and that there was no reason she should be failing. The teacher was puzzled because nothing seemed to motivate Mary. 'It's like she's had an anaesthetic. She seems to be withdrawn from anything we do', commented her teacher. She had been seen by a psychiatrist who was sure she had childhood depression and recommended drugs, but Mary's mother didn't believe in drugs. She had been brought up the natural way which said that you just get over things in life. You don't need drugs. Mary's mother was very intelligent too and was a high school teacher. She told me that she and Mary's father were separated and divorced when Mary was five years old but she was happy for both her children to see him when he was in town. (Mary had an older brother who was also very bright.)

When her mother had left the room, I spoke gently to Melancholic Mary. 'Tell me, I said what does it feel like when you have to do work in school?' She looked at me wistfully and replied: 'I can't do work in school any more because when I look at the board or the worksheets my mind is full of "blurry stuff" so I can't think. I have to copy from the kid next to me and I don't know why I can't think any more'. I looked deeply into her beautiful soft hazel eyes and saw all the signs of sadness: the lack of lustre, the shadow, the heaviness of even a smile. 'Mary,' I said, 'I think we need to have a look into your heart. I'm certain it could tell us why you can't think any more. How about you use your x-ray eyes and imagine stepping into your heart. I want you to draw all the shapes and colours that you see in it'. Mary courageously stepped into her heart, and then drew her heart. It was red with a big jagged black line down the middle. 'It looks broken Mary, how about you step into the black line and tell me what you see and feel inside the black line in your heart,' I responded. Mary told me this story when she stepped into the black jagged line in her heart:

> I am very sad because my dad is away and I can't see my dad any more. He is working in another state and I have not seen him for nearly half a year. I write to Dad every week and he writes back but Mum only lets me write good things to Dad and happy things and she said I'm not to worry him. I need to tell him about my jewel box. It's very special because I keep all my treasures from my Dad in it. I have some pink and white everlasting wild flowers, a beautiful shell mirror, a big maroon beetle, a peacock's feather, a special white crystal stone ... these are all treasures that I love most that my dad sent me. When I am sad and miss my dad I get out my little box and open it and it reminds me of Dad and then I feel happy. I have pictures of Dad and me in it too. But at the beginning of the year my brother and his friend stole it and hid it and they won't tell me where it is. I told Mum but she said not to make a fuss about something unimportant like that and that it was only mostly full of junk, not valuable stuff. She doesn't understand that my heart is very sad because I miss my dad and now I don't have my jewel box any more, I am very, very sad. I sit and cry for my dad at night when Mum can't see because she says that there is no time for tears. We just have to get on with life. But I need my jewel box back because that's all I've got of my dad.

The tears trickled over her beautiful chestnut eyelashes, like a flood breaking its banks and sensing it was safe to cry here, she let loose and howled. I cried too, for all the hearts of children everywhere, silently bearing the family burdens of grief and loss. Mary gradually stopped crying and I noticed she was breathing deeply for the first time. Mary had already started to heal her heart because she had started breathing back into her heart. Over the sessions that followed I had her work with water colour, every day for four weeks just painting the colours of the feelings she had that day around her dad. Her mother was supportive and set up a little place in the house where Mary could paint what she felt. The paintings started out flooded by very dark colours, blacks and blues but gradually over the 28 days began to lighten up and yellows, pinks and gentle greens started to dominate. I saw Mary weekly and I showed her how to communicate with her dad through her thoughts and send hearts to him wherever he was working. We spent time just making a collage of photos of her and dad for her bedroom which she could imagine any time of the day. Mary began to smile again, and as she painted she started to write little poems to her dad, which she would read to me each session and we would keep in a special book. Within two weeks of Mary starting to paint, the teacher noticed that Mary was showing interest in tasks at school and by four weeks Mary told me the 'blurry stuff' in her head had disappeared. Then about two months into therapy Mary arrived with a very big smile. She shared her joyful story with me:

> I was thinking about Dad and how he would understand and make my brother give me back my jewel box so I wrote him a letter and told him how much I missed him and how much I loved him and would he come home and get my brother to give me back my jewel box. I did not show it to Mum because she wouldn't let me send it but I found an envelope and went to the shop and bought a stamp and addressed it to Dad myself and posted it. Well, guess what, Dad wrote back and said he is coming home to see me and get my jewel box back for me and he is going to get a job nearby, so I can see him every week. Mum was cross when she found out I had worried Dad about nothing, but she said it will be good for me to see him every week.

I probably don't need to say that Mary was dux again by the end of Year 4.

Grief and loss in the classroom: the tell tale signs

Children in the classroom suffering grief and loss are often just left to get through it, especially if their grief and loss does not express itself through anger or disrupt the classroom. It is as though they are not a pressing issue for classroom management unless of course in the rare cases where the child weeps several times a day and is unable to complete class work. I would argue that children in today's world are assaulted by grief and loss on a regular basis: loss of homes and friends through the highly mobile family, losses through marriage breakdowns, illness of their own or their parents, loss of pets, deaths of loved ones, loss of safety in their lives and loss of spaces for innocent childhood play and joy. The losses are cumulative in children today. Grief and loss is also very complex because at times there is guilt as well. Young children, particularly in the five to six age group, may also believe that in some way they are responsible for the death or the loss.

Children who are having serious problems with grief and loss may show one or more of these signs:

- an extended period of depression in which the child loses interest in daily activities and events
- an inability to sleep, a loss of appetite, a prolonged fear of being alone
- acting younger for an extended period
- excessively imitating the dead person (in the case of a death)
- repeated statements of wanting to join the dead person (particularly if a parent)
- withdrawal from friends
- sharp drop in school performance or refusal to attend school. (American Academy of Child and Adolescent Psychiatry 2004)

If serious grief and loss is ignored over extended periods, it can become a core foundation for childhood depression, which is escalating at alarming rates in the western world. Emotional literacy in our classrooms must teach children skills to recover joy for their lives, so that the grief and loss can be digested and not cumulate into anomie or depression.

Current models for managing grief and loss in primary school children

While sensitive empathetic teachers recognise children in grief and loss and 'make allowances for them', most teachers are not trained to manage grief to the extent that they are trained to manage anger. Usually if the child shows severe symptoms they will be referred to the school psychologist who will listen to the child's story but lack the languages of emotional literacy. In Australia, the school psychologist will be cognitively behaviourally trained and probably use a desensitisation approach or a reinforcement behavioural program. If these are unsuccessful, the child will usually be referred to a psychiatrist who may diagnose childhood depression and recommend a drug program. The side effects of drugging children and adolescents for depression are of deep concern to many health professionals. These drugs have serious impacts on the immature body. In 2004, the British Medical Association after reviewing the side effects of drugs for depression on adolescents and children banned the use of SSRIs (anti depressants) on adolescents and children (Herxheimer 2004.) They were withdrawn by the committee dealing with safety in medicine and health care products (Murray et al 2004). Increasingly research is signalling the serious overuse of drugs on children and adolescents for mental health conditions. Burke (2007) alerts us to the serious problem of the enmeshed relationships between the pharmaceutical industry and academic medical researchers and the Food and Drug Administration (FDA) in the USA, which is resulting in inaccurate or premature data on drug trials on children. Burke cites the work of Safer (2002) and Nielson (2003) that shows that drug industry sponsored research tends to yield findings that support the drug industry's agenda. Greenhill (2003) argues for the need for longer drug trials. Cohen and Jacobs (2007) argue that randomised controlled trials lose their validity when they focus on 'made up psychiatric diagnostic categories' and scientifically debunk much of the research of efficacy of antidepressant drugs concluding that

the backdrop is American biopsychiatry's insistence that personal difficulties must be viewed as the expression of idiopathic somatic diseases and the pharmaceutical industry's dominance of the entire drug treatment research enterprise.

Day (2002) highlights the hazards of the current trend to over 'psychiatrise' children, adolescents and adults and points out that in 1968, the DSM II (*Diagnostic and statistical manual of mental disorders*) listed 163 mental health disorders which escalated to 374 in 1994 with the release of the DSM-R IV (*Diagnostic and statistical manual of mental disorders revised*). A whole new raft of mental health illnesses applicable to children and adolescents were created in this time.

There is a trend among some psychiatrists and some psychologists to diagnose children with childhood depression and suggest drugs, when in most of the cases working with the grief and loss will free up the natural healing rhythms in the child's body, heart and mind and the child can naturally return to wellbeing. Drugging and labelling also become seriously prone to misuse by parents, mental health professionals and authorities who themselves lack the skills of emotional literacy. Rather than confront their inadequacy to relate to the child from the heart, they act from the sterile hallway of cognitive supremacy and deal with challenging behaviours by controlling the child's will and personality or by repressing it with drugs. The ADHD drug treatment program is a case in point. Alternative child empowering non-drug interventions like the 'extra lesson' focus on restoring the natural rhythms of body, heart and mind, cultivate the languages of emotional literacy and have outstanding academic and social results while maintaining the child's dignity, personality, will and physical wellbeing (Opening the Door 2001). Diet, particularly constraints around excess sugar and artificial additives assist the behaviour of many children with ADHD diagnosis as do various behaviour management processes (Block 1996). However, these take time, patience and a commitment to work heart to heart with the child.

Body-based holistic classroom interventions for managing grief and loss

The body-based holistic approach integrating the body, heart and mind of the child offers insights to the teacher in addressing grief and loss in the classroom. It recognises the teacher is not a therapist and that the heart of the classroom withers when the grief and loss of children is ignored, repressed or denied. It advocates simple emotional literacy exercises to enable children to breathe through grief and loss in the classroom so that it does not need to become depression. If the child can continue to breathe through the grief and loss experience, neither ignoring it nor suppressing it, then the heart of the child will continue to flourish and the classroom becomes a flourishing learning and supportive social environment.

(a) whole class exercises

Grief and loss is often a whole class experience. Examples are loss of a loved headmaster after several years of leadership, loss of a loved teacher who is transferred to another school, loss of a student peer who leaves the school, group loss that is triggered by loss of a parent by one member of the class, and loss of a peer or a significant sporting event.

Group exercise 1:
watercolour for working to heal a grief and loss experience

Materials
- Watercolour paper: 3 sheets per child
- Watercolour paints at least red, yellow, blue, black, and green
- Paintbrushes: one large and one medium for each child
- Water and jars
- Paint palette (can use lids of ice cream containers)

Step 1   Ask the children to place a hand on the part of their body in which they feel the most sadness when they think about the loss.

Step 2   Ask the children to wet the first sheet of paper with water then to drop colours onto the water that represents how the sadness in their body is feeling.

Step 3   Take the second sheet of paper and this time ask the children to again paint 'wet on wet' the quality they have lost as a result of the loss, that is, joy, friendships, happiness, fun, love. As they paint the missing quality have them imagine they are breathing this quality into the part of their body that is feeling most sad.

Step 4   Take the third sheet of paper. Ask them to put their hand back on their bodies where they felt the sadness before and with their x-ray eyes have a look at the colours and shapes in that part of the body. Paint the colours and shapes.

The third painting will represent a combination of the colours and shapes in Paintings 1 and 2. The more the colours resemble Painting 2, the closer the move to healing the grief. This exercise can be repeated easily for one week, each day selecting another lost quality to paint. Each day the three paintings are completed as specified above. By the final day of the week, the last painting should resemble a movement away from grief and a restoration of positive feeling and breath. This is evidenced by the lightening up of colours used in the painting, more flow in the lines of the colours and more directive energy rather than blobs of colour. The children can also explore how they can bring more fun, friends, warmth, joy or whatever the missing quality is they identified, into their day-to-day lives.

Group exercise 2:
removing the shock arising from a grief and loss experience

Whenever the grief and loss experience was unexpected, sudden or unpredictable, the child will experience it as a 'shock'. This shock affects the rhythmic system of the child, throwing it off balance by contracting the breathing where the shock is lodged in the child's body. Every child can tell you where in their body the shock is stuck. Most often with children it is stuck in the heart or the stomach.

Step 1   Ask the children where in their body the shock of hearing about the loss is stuck.

Step 2   Get each child to step forwards into their body where the shock is stuck and describe how the shock is stuck in them: Is it like a knife, a sword, something twisted inside of them or like a lump of wood stuck inside them?

Step 3	Ask them to pull out the dagger or sword or knife with a sound which goes from contracted breathing to expanded breathing such as nnnnnn to aarrrhh, or uuuuu to haaah.
Step 4	Ask the children to breathe back a beautiful colour into the part of the body where the shock was held. Have the children move about and with a gesture and a sound feel the quality that makes this part of their body feel happy.

It is essential that the senses are engaged in recovery of all emotional trauma. We must experience through the senses the new patterns of positive life and energy. It cannot just be done with words. Beard and Wilson (2006) in their inspiring book, *Experiential Learning* document the importance of multi-sensory engagement in the learning process that is to be transformative for the child. It is critical in the transformation of negative emotional experiences into positive experiences.

Group exercise 3:
watercolour sequence for grief: creating a ritual to honour the person or thing that has been lost

Step 1	Enter back into the place of the body that is the site of grief but has now received the qualities it needs to recover. Focus on how the qualities are healing in that part of the body. Paint in watercolour (wet paint on wet paper) the healing place in the body.
Step 2	Create a ritual using the healing place drawn in watercolour to honour the potential of the relationship or the attribute of the person. This may be done in many ways but must involve the body in the activity. It could involve planting a flower garden to honour the person, it may be painting a tree, or painting and framing a painting that honours the person, completing a collage of happy memories using photographs, sewing a mural with patches made by each student to honour the person who has been lost, writing a poem about them or making up a play.

(b)   Individual exercises: introducing the grief and loss healing corner in the classroom

Once the whole class is familiar with how to work with grief and loss to bring back happiness and joy, you can introduce them to the grief and loss healing corner in the classroom. This centre has a table with watercolour supplies and watercolour paper. Whenever a child has a particular grief and loss issue or is just feeling sad without knowing why, they can go to the grief and loss healing corner and take themselves through the watercolour painting process outlined in Group exercise 1 above. This then becomes a self-motivated process with students demonstrating their capacity to identify when they are in grief and loss and take the initiative to restore happiness back to themselves.

Case study

Robert was eleven years old and was very sad that he could not play with his friends any longer after school because the playing fields where they had played soccer had been closed down. He was an only child and he felt stuck at home by himself. We followed the grief and loss sequence in watercolour and his three drawings opposite illustrate the healing process.

Following this work we thought about ways he could do things in his life that would increase his happiness and he concluded he would like to join a soccer team so he had friends to play sport with after school and on weekends and he would ask his mother if this was okay. The energy in his whole body awoke, his lethargy disappeared and a new light came back into his eyes as he realised that he did not have to be stuck in his grief and loss but could find pathways through it to create other times of happiness. It is important that the change in his breathing and body that is achieved by the watercolour work is completed as well as the external changes. Otherwise only half of the issue is addressed. It is critical children learn to change their inner feeling life because it is not always possible to change external conditions. They need to learn to be happy even when they cannot always have the friends or things that they want. This is an important life skill for adulthood as well. Inner contentment can never be achieved simply with the manipulation of external conditions.

Painting 1 The sadness at not having a friend to play with after school

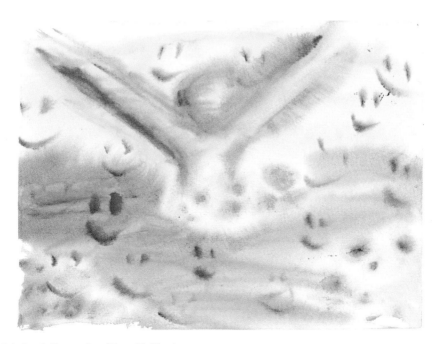

Painting 2 The quality of fun with friends

Painting 3 How breathing in the quality of fun has changed the sadness to happiness

Conclusion

If children learn ways to identify sadness affecting their heart, body and mind and skills to help bring back happiness and joy, then we are cultivating a classroom where the flowers of the heart will grow in rich soil and bear beautiful perfumed flowers. It will also give the children ongoing skills to help them have a greater heart space in their homes. As adults, they will enter the workplace and the world with skills to negotiate a pathway through grief and loss experiences that can keep open the doorway to hope and joy. You, as a teacher, will have taught an essential life skill that they can use to find the silver lining in every cloud and create pathways from grief and loss back to hope and joy.

References

American Academy of Child and Adolescent Psychiatry 2004, *Children and grief.* Accessed 22 May 2007 at www.aacap.org/page.ww?section=Facts+for+Families&name=Children+And+Grief

Beard, C & Wilson, J 2006, *Experiential learning: A best practice handbook for educators and trainers*, 2nd edn, Kogan Page, London.

Block, MA (1996), *No more ritalin: Treating ADHD children without drugs*, Kensington Publishing Corp., London.

Burke, MG 2007, 'Commentary by a child psychiatrist practicing in a community setting', *Journal of Child and Adolescent Psychopharmacology*, vol. 17, no. 3, pp. 295–9.

Cohen, D & Jacobs, DH 2007, 'Randomized controlled trials of antidepressants: Clinically and scientifically irrelevant', *Debates in Neuroscience*, vol. 1, no. 1, pp. 44–54.

Day, P 2002, *The mind game*, Credence Publications, Kent, UK.

Greenhill, L 2003, 'Introduction: Assessment of safety in pediatric psychopharmacology', *Journal of the American Academy of Child and Adolescent Psychiatry*, vol. 42, no. 6, pp. 625–6.

Herxheimer, A 2004, 'Treating major depression in children and adolescents: Use of selective serotonin reuptake inhibitors needs urgent clarification' (letter), *British Medical Journal,* vol. 328, p. 524.

Murray, M, Wong, I & De Vris, C (2004), 'Treating major depression in children and adolescents' (letter), *British Medical Journal,* vol. 328, pp. 524–5.

Opening the Door 2001, *Extra lesson*. Accessed 22 February 2008 at www.opening-the-door.com/ext_less.htm

*His heart was like a sensitive plant, that opens
for a moment in the sunshine, but curls up and
shrinks into itself at the slightest touch of the
finger, or the lightest breath of wind.*

Anne Brontë (1858)

CHAPTER 5

Fear: braving the storm

Stomach ache Susan did not want to go to school because it gave her stomach aches, especially first thing in the day. Susan was seven years old and it did not matter whether she ate Cornflakes, Weet-bix or muesli for breakfast, she always had a stomach ache so badly that she just could not concentrate on her morning work at school. Every day she asked the teacher to send her home because she was sick. The doctor said there was nothing wrong with Susan, and that it was all in her imagination. The teacher said it was psychological and Susan's mother was too sick to be too concerned because she was in her second year of chemotherapy treatment for her breast cancer. No one at school remembered when her stomach aches had begun. It was as though they were part of Susan just like her nose or her mouth. Then one day Susan ran away from school and walked one kilometre home. Her mother was most upset that something might have happened to her with all the busy roads she had crossed alone and so it came to the attention of the principal that Susan needed psychological help. When I first saw Susan I was impressed by her fineness of being, her slight fairy-like build and her soft liquid voice. All she needed was a wand to transform her into the fairy queen. It wasn't surprising that she loved fairies and had personal conversations with the fairy queen on the way to the fairy ball to which she was always invited. Susan had pretty blonde hair that vibrated in the sunlight when she shook her head, which she did often. She was clearly the sensitive type, somewhat nervous and definitely underweight. She hugged a tattered fairy teddy, battered with her love. Her fear was clearly palpable in her liquid blue eyes that flickered with uncertainty and she clutched her stomach with one hand. 'Susan,' I said, 'we're going to find out what's going wrong in your heart that is giving you stomach aches'. Then I asked her to literally take a step forward into her stomach and with her x-ray eyes look for the shapes and colours inside it. Then I asked Susan to step backwards out of her stomach and draw these shapes and colours for me. She drew a black ball in the middle, green squirmy worm-like shapes floating around and big chunks of triangular brown stuff also floating around the black in her stomach. Then I asked Susan to step into the black ball with her whole body and tell me what she was feeling when she stepped into it. Susan found herself in a place where she felt abandoned and was very frightened. I asked her why it was so scary in there and she said because she was alone and her mum could not come to help her because she was so sick. When I asked Susan to step into the green squirmy worms in her drawing, she said she felt really scared in there because when she was in there she felt that her mother was going to die and she would be left all alone with her baby brother Timothy. When Susan stepped into the brown chunks floating around in her stomach she said she was worried that she could not help her mum enough to get better because she was too small and she could not help her when she was at school. It was very clear that Susan was fearful that her mother would die while she was away at school and the fear was lying in her stomach, blocking the free flow of her energy and her digestion. It was obvious why Susan did not want to go to school. Susan and I did several sessions together but the most important qualities Susan needed to heal were courage, strength and support. She painted in watercolour a beautiful fairy queen with lots of fairy assistants who were to come and live with her in the black hole and who could do magic so that they could turn the black hole into a happy place. They could also bring good health to help her mother get better. As soon as Susan realised she did not have to be alone with her problem and that we could bring persons, human and fairy, to help us through hard times, her fear levels started to drop. Once the black hole was peopled with courage and hope, the green squiggly things disappeared. After speaking to Susan's mother, she agreed to a network of home visitors and helpers which was set up through the school parents. When Susan realised other people were visiting her mother during the day even the brown chunky bits in her stomach disappeared and with that her stomach aches. Strong Susan, who now had courage in her heart in place of fear, went back to school and began to flourish. She won the monthly award for making shining progress in her school work. But most importantly, Susan learned that in a crisis your magic wand is friends, visible and invisible, otherwise fear can become your constant companion and fear just makes you weak and sick. Susan explained to me: 'When the fairy queen asks me to the fairy ball, I need to feel happy. Otherwise I just don't wear my prettiest clothes'.

Fear in the heart of the classroom

Unless the teacher has a style that is intimidating to the students, then fear in the classroom tends to come in a wave and the heart of the classroom becomes shaky. A wave of fear may come through the death of a peer, a serious accident of a peer, the death of a teacher or the death of another child's parent. Fear may come from a natural disaster involving some of the school community. An example was the collapse of the beach cliffs during the school end of the year picnic in the community of Gracetown, WA, which resulted in the deaths of a teacher and some students. Whatever the cause of the fear, it cannot be ignored. In traumatic group events the education department may provide counselling to debrief a critical incident, but bureaucracies do not have a good reputation at effective grass-roots interventions and despite good intentions, may not accurately identify the correct issue or the cause of the fear or grief and loss. I remember two eight-year-olds recalling the following experience after all the children in the school were given notes by the education department suggesting they could ask for counselling if they were worried or frightened by the principal's death through cancer:

> Why do they offer us help now? We never knew Mr X (the principal who had died of cancer) because he stayed in his office all the time and he never spoke to us. But when our hearts were broken when they moved Mr Y (the previous child-centred principal who had great personal relationships with

every child) to a different school after he had loved us for three years, no one offered us counselling.

Helping children as a group move through fears and assisting children individually move from fear to courage is the gift the teacher can bring to support the health of the heart of the classroom. What follows in this chapter provides the key tools and understandings a teacher can use to facilitate this transition.

Current models of the management of fear in the classroom

Currently teachers have no specific training to manage fear in the classroom. Fear identification and management must be a major aspect of emotional literacy. It is another of those emotions largely denied or repressed unless there is a major critical incident. Consequently children are often left to live with fears and teachers feel unskilled to address them. Of course if an individual child develops extreme attacks of fear, that is, panic attacks, then usually they will be referred to the school psychologist who will apply a cognitive behavioural management program, which can mean desensitisation. If this fails then referral to a psychiatrist and drugging will often be recommended. Panic attacks in children can be addressed easily and rapidly in this model of holistic body-based therapy, within 1–4 sessions and usually entirely eliminated, without drugs. While panic attacks and acute fears like phobias remain the province of professional therapists, basic fears of children in the classroom can be well managed by the teacher as part of emotional literacy to create a courageous heart of the classroom.

Body-based holistic model for understanding fear in children

The first thing the teacher needs to understand about fear is that it is an unhelpful feeling that needs to be exited as soon as possible. A simple technique developed by Tagar which he named the 'bamboo sequence'

(Sherwood 2004) facilitates the exit of the fear experience within one minute. This can be done with an individual or a group and is outlined in Group exercise 1 below. As a teacher you can practise this simple technique on your own fears to see how remarkably effective it is. It is important that the 'g' (gh … gh … gh) sound is made loudly, as if the 'g' was bouncing on the wall upon which the fear is being thrown out of the body. Remember the 'g' restores the flow of the breath through the bodily system and in fear we radically constrict our flow of breath. Fear needs to be released so the breath and the natural healthy heart rhythms can return fully to their body.

The other core understanding that is observable phenomenologically is that there is a part of the mind of children; the highest part that can be called the child's spirit or insight or self-awareness, which keeps them feeling powerful and safe in their lives. It leaves their body when they feel powerless and are in fear. It carries the memory of events as well the child's full presence. One can observe this in the body language of a child and we might describe it as 'daydreaming' or 'not concentrating'. So, for example, the child's physical body is in the classroom, their eyes are open, and they may even talk to you but their higher mind is not there. When this happens we label the child as 'distracted' and 'not paying attention'. Adults do it too, but in children it occurs much more frequently. Children may do this when they are bored, tired or simply unmotivated to learn something. Almost all children will do so when they feel unsafe or fearful. Children do this in stages. The first stage is shaking legs or feet as the breath leaves and with it carries the presence of the higher mind. If the fear continues to mount then we have Stage 2 where it will move to the abdomen and the feeling of needing to go to the toilet arises. In Stage 3, the fear moves up to the stomach and children will say they have 'butterflies in the stomach' or feel like vomiting. At this stage, the breath is very contracted. By Stage 4, the breath is contracted in the throat and at this point the person often feels unable to breathe properly and may have panic attacks. When the breath is so constricted that it is contracted through the forehead, the person feels dizzy (Stage 5). If the higher mind leaves the body entirely then the child will faint as may happen in the case of severe shock. I have had several cases of children being bullied at school who faint from fear when the bully approaches them. These children leave their body so quickly in the face of fear that they faint. The antidote to this process of the higher mind leaving the body is to teach the child to return consciously to the body. Unless the higher mind is in the body, the child does not have the power to confront the fear and eliminate it. The teacher can assist children to conquer fear by teaching them 'grounding', which is outlined in the exercise below. These exercises of 'bamboo' and 'grounding' are also applicable to children in states of extreme anger or rage (Group exercises 1 and 2 below).

Body-based holistic classroom interventions for transforming fear into courage

Group exercise 1:
bamboo—exiting the fear quickly

Step 1	Ask the children to place their hands on the part of the body where they feel the fear.
Step 2	Ask the children to collect the fear into a ball.
Step 3	Ask them to throw the fear away from their body making the sound 'g' (gh ... gh ... gh) out loud.
Step 4	Suggest to the children that they step backwards and out of that part of their body.
Step 5	Tell them to shake off the fear energy with their hands.
Step 6	Repeat Steps 2–5 until no fear is felt any more in any part of their body.

Group exercise 2:
returning to the body—grounding

The easiest way to get children to return to their body AFTER completing the bamboo sequence is to have them stamp both feet on the ground and walk around the room saying out loud in unison with the steps of their feet:

'I am here, I am safe, I am here, I am safe'. As the child stamps their feet strongly on the ground the breath is forced back into the feet and legs. Running a few laps around the school oval will achieve the same outcome, and that is why many teachers intuitively know that when children become ragged, irritable and moody that a run around the school oval restores the natural rhythms of the body-heart-mind through deep breathing. Children return to the classroom after such a run, more centred and literally with the breath moving through their body.

Group resource exercises

It is critical to understand that a child can only confront a fear using resources drawn from the human, animal, plant or archetypal worlds that resonate with the child as protective figures and which they can place between themselves and their fear. Exercises for developing these resources, which will become a critical foundation for the child's adult resources, are listed below. They are to be highly recommended as resources that can assist children to protect and nurture their hearts and their feeling lives in the face of life's challenges and difficult conditions. (This is not to suggest that children should be left in abusive situations and given resources only. Here institutional intervention is required.) All teachers can help children accessing resources to keep their hearts healthy, safe and flourishing. Appropriate exercises are identified below (Group exercises 3, 4, 5, 6).

Group exercise 3:
creating a class resource folder

The core idea here is to explore with the class images that give the child a sense of protection and safety and collect these into a personal resource folder. A plastic sleeve book is ideal for this exercise.

Step 1   Each child chooses images of the earth, such as mountains, Uluru and other great rocks that they feel give them a sense of protection and safety.

Step 2   Each child chooses plant images like forests or great oak trees that give them a sense of power, protection and safety.

Step 3   Each child chooses animal images that give them a sense of protection and safety. Animal images are the most common images of protection selected by primary school children and these will include images of lions, elephants, good dragons, certain dogs, and the like.

Step 4   Other images include both visible and invisible figures such as Mum, Dad, a particular relative, Superman, St George, St Michael and for some children religious figures like Jesus, Buddha, Ganesha.

Each child contributes at least one image from the earth, plants, animals and/or personal figures to their file that is meaningful to them and which increases their feelings of safety and strength in the face of fear. They may draw these images or cut out pictures of them. The child can add to this resource folder throughout the year. These images are bigger than the child's fear and can protect them from it. Tacey (2003) points out the critical need for young people to have connections to images beyond themselves arguing that this connectedness is a powerful buffer against powerlessness, alienation and aloneness. This resource file is a prerequisite for Group exercise 4.

Group exercise 4:
resourcing the protective guard

This exercise is most appropriate when there is a general feeling of fear in the classroom among the children.

Step 1   Each child senses where in the body they feel the fear, for example, the stomach.

Step 2   Each child selects a particular resource from the resource folder that they feel can protect them from the fear.

Step 3   The child draws the image on a very large sheet of paper. It is important that the image is large. The child colours in the image with chalks, crayons or paint.

Step 4   The child imagines receiving courage and power from this image.

Step 5   The child breathes this courage and power into the part of the body where they felt the fear and gives the breath a colour so they can keep track of it. Here coloured material scarves or large pieces of fabric are wonderful as the child can select the required coloured piece of fabric and wrap it around themselves.

Step 6   The child gestures the new strength in their body and walks around the room feeling powerful and courageous.

Step 7   The child finds a strong sound to accompany the gesture usually earth sounds like 'b', 'd', or 'g' which give the child a feeling of strength.

Step 8   The child draws themselves in the gesture of strength and courage surrounded by the guard or protector.

This drawing is then placed on their desk to remind them that they have the courage to overcome the fear.

Group exercise 5:
protecting oneself from fear—clay work

This exercise is also increasing the child's capacity to feel safe and strong in face of the fear.

Materials
- Working size board usually about half a metre by half a metre or plastic sheeting to cover work tables.
- A water spray bottle.
- An airtight bucket of standard pottery clay in one of the earth hues.
- Towel for cleaning hands
- Three to four good hand-sized balls of clay

Step 1: the site of the fear
- Sense where in their body, the children feel the fear.
- Make the shape of the fear in clay.

Step 2: the force of the fear
- Ask the children to make in clay how they feel the force of the fear is attacking them. Is it like arrows, stones, a steamroller, etc.?

Step 3: the guard that can protect them from the fear
- Ask the child to make a powerful image that can protect them from the fear, for example, big warrior, a big angel, a big shield, a lion, etc.
- Ask them to place the clay image between themselves and the force of the fear.

Step 4: the courageous one who can stand up in the face of the fear
- Ask the children to make a courageous strong image of themselves that can stand up against the fear.
- Keep this clay image of themselves as a powerful tool on their desks.

Group exercise 6:
enlarging light in pictures

Here you ask the children to paint or complete a coloured drawing of how they are feeling about the situation of fear. In the drawing there is usually one place in which the colours are light. Especially, look for the yellow or gold or clear green or light blue colours. Ask the children to imagine magnifying what is inside the yellow or gold and make a big picture of what is inside this place. This will reveal the child's innate resources to cope with the fear and by painting the images large, they are enlarged in the child's body, heart and mind. The magnified images empower the child with courage to deal with difficult situations.

Individual exercises: establishing the resourcing corner of the classroom

Once the above exercises have been completed by the whole class, you are ready to establish a resource corner of the classroom where the resource folder will be kept, as well as some clay and a clay board, coloured crayons and big sheets of drawing paper. If a child is feeling fearful they can self-direct or be directed to the resource corner of the classroom. Here they can exit their fear and ground themselves, then choose to undertake one of Exercises 3, 4, 5 or 6. Images of protection made by the child should always be kept and not destroyed.

Resourcing restores the colour, the light, the joy, the dignity to children and gives them the opportunity to hold onto connectedness to hope, despite difficult conditions around them. Resourcing work is core for working with children as they respond to it with enthusiasm, and make major leaps in their confidence and the capacity to deal with difficult issues in their lives. When resourcing with children, the more creative, the bigger the symbols, and the more active the artistic activities, the more effective the energetic transformation. In essence, resourcing provides an experiential process engaging the senses that transforms difficult experiences into manageable challenges and opportunities for growth and skill development. As Beard and Wilson (2006) indicate:

> The more senses we use in an activity the more memorable the learning experience will become because it increases the neural connections in our brains and will therefore be more accessible.

Developmentally children under seven are in touch with imagination, fantasy and the magic of the pre-operational world and respond to resourcing with vibrancy and enthusiasm. It is as though they are still embraced in a childhood spirituality, from which emerges a natural and spontaneous connectivity. Even in some of the most traumatised little children, it is as though they are waiting for the door to their spirit of hope to be opened again, to be acknowledged and renewed. A profound experience of using artistic resources to assist a four-year-old child in an oncology treatment ward in a children's hospital is recounted by Birch (1997). The fear and terror of the treatment room was countered by enlarging the child's resources, the teddy, the safe island, the beach, the sunshine, the bird and the place that the child could go to find peace and tranquillity in the face of the invasive painful treatment program.

Case study

The Year 3 students at Good Child primary school had a very well-meaning teacher who wanted to teach them about the hazards of watching adult videos. She had an article from the newspaper that spoke of a young primary school child in the USA who had ended up in psychiatric services after watching the R-rated video with her parents. She had photocopied the cover of the video and distributed it to the children with the newspaper article. The cover of the video had a face screaming in a sadistic gesture. The class did not view any part of the video but the next day several parents complained that their children showed a range of fear behaviours including refusing to go to sleep, not wanting to leave the parent or being fearful of being alone. One of these children presented in my counselling rooms. The child's fears were tracked back to the video cover the children had seen in school. Group exercises 4, 5 and 6 were essential in helping this child overcome fear, and regain courage and strength. The protective images drawn and made in clay were taken home and it was suggested that they be placed in the child's bedroom. The child recovered his sense of confidence and safety in his world as the positive images he had created now substantially outweighed the negative sadistic image. The child had resources to protect him from his fear and to keep him safe.

Conclusion

Fear weakens all of us, children and adults alike, and reduces our capacity to follow our hearts and live from our truth and strength in the world. The gift teachers give children in mastering their fears and restoring their strength and courage in the classroom empowers them for life so they can see that they have choices about how they respond to the challenges that come their way. It is a life skill of the most precious order. It gives them courage to create a space to keep breathing their truth and to know that they do not have to face life's fears alone. There are long-term personal and social rewards from schooling for emotional literacy.

References

Beard, C & Wilson, JP 2006, *Experiential learning: A best practice book for educators and trainers*, 2nd edn, Kogan Page, London.

Birch, L 1997, 'Fortifying the healing process: Art therapy for children with cancer', in I Gawler (ed.) *Science, passion and healing: The relationship between mind, immunity and health*, The Gawler Foundation, Melbourne.

Brontë, A 1858, *The tenant of Wildfell Hall*, Harper & Brothers Publishers, Franklin Square, New York.

Sherwood, P 2004, *The healing art of clay therapy*, ACER Press, Melbourne.

Tacey, D 2003, *The spirituality revolution: The emergence of contemporary spirituality*, Harper Collins, Sydney.

Once I knew only darkness and stillness ...
my life was without past or future ... but a little
word from the fingers of another fell into my
hand that clutched at emptiness, and my heart
leaped to the rapture of living.

Helen Keller (2003)

CHAPTER 6

Aloneness: filling holes in the heart

Miserable Matilda was one of the saddest 10-year-olds I had ever met. She had deep brown eyes that looked like they were forest pools flooding with unshed tears. She was pale and wane with a withdrawn, listless energy in her body. Matilda had come to counselling because she had jumped off the roof of the school shed and although she was not physically hurt, she said she was trying to kill herself and that 'life was so hard she did not want to live any more'. Miserable Matilda was very slow to speak and even drawing pictures was a labour. I could see she had the gentlest nature, like a young shy gazelle, and the softest heart, and was really overwhelmed by her life's experiences. Her mum had died when she was five years old. Mum had suicided and dad had found Matilda sitting next to her when he came home from work. Dad had remarried a year later to a woman who was strong and dominating and ran the household with military precision, like the general of an army. Matilda had rostered jobs or homework from the moment of waking to the moment of sleeping. Matilda believed her stepmother hated her. Her stepmother was a well-meaning lady and told me that she was doing the best she could 'to prepare Matilda for life in the world, so that she did not turn out to be hopeless, like her mother'. The aloneness of Matilda's heart was overwhelming. She could not relate to her stepmother and her father was a salesman, and often away from home. When at home, he was busy helping with the two new children in the family, one who was six months old and the other who was two years old. Although she loved her father, she felt cut off from his heart because she had no time to be with him or talk to him. Her stepmother forbade her to talk about her mother and she felt utterly abandoned emotionally. Matilda survived by a shoestring of connection to her dead mother which she described:

> Under my mattress I hide a picture of my mother. At night when I go to bed I get it out and I talk to her and tell her how sad my heart is and how much I miss her. She told me she loves me and to come and join her ... that's why I was jumping off the school shed roof so I would die and go to be with my mother.

Aloneness was killing Matilda. Aloneness whose grandfather and grandmother is grief and loss, and whose father and mother is emotional abandonment. Aloneness chills the heart of children and when the heart starts to freeze the child gives up on life. I knew Matilda needed warmth to flood back into her little heart so she could recover the joys of life. Clearly, her father was the one source of warmth she had in this world to which she needed to be reconnected. I called her stepmother and father in for a session together about 'how best to support Matilda'. I strongly suggested dad needed to have special time just with Matilda for one hour per week, talking to her and doing fun things with her. Matilda's stepmother said that she was just frazzled with the responsibility of running the household and the worries about Matilda's future. She was delighted with the idea of a self-responsibility plan that she, Matilda and I would develop together and which gave Matilda more freedom to direct her own life, decide what she would eat, and that made spaces for her play time. The family budget could stretch to an adult home helper two hours a week which freed Matilda from many of the daily chores and gave stepmum reliable adult support to help with the children. The stepmother was so unhappy that she had no time for herself, so she adopted the suggestion that one afternoon a week she claim back time for herself. Then I talked about Matilda's need to have a space in her room to honour her mother and to be able to freely talk about her. Dad and stepmum had been well meaning in banning talk about her because they thought it was bad for Matilda. However, together with Matilda, they learned that for psychological health she needed to breathe through her grief and loss, not repress or deny it. Matilda stayed on to do several sessions to learn the languages of emotional literacy and to work around her grief and loss, and her need to reconnect with warmth and love. Special time with dad worked like magic, and when I checked in with Matilda six months down the track she had a new light in her eyes and a new warmth in her heart. She told me how much she loved time with her dad, that her stepmother was sort of kinder now and that she had allowed her to have a puppy which she just adored. Matilda's story is just one example of how dark aloneness can become for a child. Early intervention by teaching children the languages of emotional literacy is essential so they can express their needs before a possible tragedy occurs.

Aloneness in the heart of the classroom

Children need heart warmth to flourish in their bodies, minds and hearts. Post-war research into orphans in institutions showed that even when meeting all the physical needs, children fail to flourish physically, mentally and emotionally if they are not given loving attention. Children's growth is hampered by aloneness which chills their hearts and leaves them in a state of cold abandonment. In our classrooms today there are children in many degrees of aloneness and emotional coldness. They may have physical affluence but their hearts are hungry for loving warm connectedness. Every early primary teacher knows the signs of these children. They cling to your body, legs, arms or hands; whatever part of you they feel might radiate loving warmth to them. The hunger for emotional warmth is in their eyes. Some children call attention to their need for loving warm connection through 'attention seeking behaviours' because at least they are getting some connection, even without the warmth. Some children act out with aggressive behaviours towards other children who they experience as competing for the little warmth there is in their lives. Unfortunately today, families are busy, often with both parents working long hours, grandparents on the other side of the country, and no close relatives living nearby. This is often compounded by frequent shifts of residence to follow the promotion trails across the country or the next lucrative job offer. Surprisingly, given deep heart warmth children can flourish emotionally as much in a tent or a transportable house as in an expensive architect designed house or condominium. Parents often try to replace the time they do not spend with their children with toys and things, but these are a temporary filler and a poor substitute for emotional warmth. So many children come to school hungering for connectedness, warmth, and its companion—understanding. Just listen to the six-year-olds' round of news that they tell the teacher. So often they speak of their fears and their worries that threaten their sense of secure connection and love. 'Dad hit Mum last night and we packed our suitcase and left', 'Mum has a boyfriend and Dad was angry and shouted at her', 'Mum is busy with the new baby and I don't get bedtime stories any more', 'Mum is sick and I'm scared she might die', 'Mum is in hospital and I don't like the baby sitter'. Teachers whose hearts are awake often grieve daily and their arms feel as though they are not big enough to surround and hold the needs of these children. Many teachers feel they need to push on and meet all the curriculum outcomes when providing an environment that teaches children skills of the languages of emotional literacy and how to transform aloneness is more essential. As Goleman (1996) reiterates, it is our emotional intelligence that determines our achievements in life not our cognitive intelligence. Such feelings of abandonment, the inability to name the feeling, let alone find ways to transform it, is the foundation for many types of adolescent and adult addictions. The lack of emotional literacy in our schools is costing us all too much.

Body-based holistic model for understanding feelings of aloneness in children

In a body-based holistic model, connectedness to meaningful others, the great antidote to aloneness, is seen as a core emotional need for children. It is through connectedness that the child finds nourishment in the world for their feeling life. When the feeling life is warmed then all the life forces flow better and there is greater physical wellbeing and more availability for learning. Lievegoed (1997) notes the critical nature of connectedness between the developing self of the child and their ability to absorb what is happening in the world around them. He identifies stage 1 which is the milk teeth stage usually from about 0–7 years when the child has a great openness to the outer world and assimilates almost everything in their environment. They have a natural connectedness with life and the self is not defined strongly. During this period, it is essential that there is much heart warmth so the child can experience sufficient safety in their life forces that they continue to want to incarnate more fully in the world. During the second phase from 7–12, the child's sense of self becomes more contained as the child attempts to conquer the outside world and has to digest and assimilate the experiences that come to them. However, the child becomes unhappy when experiences enter that they can no longer assimilate and these are often isolated and repressed and emerge later in the adult life to cause unhappiness. A warm environment in which the child experiences connectedness with a significant adult enables them to process these experiences, thus paving the way for a happier and emotionally healthier adulthood. The teacher is in a position to help the child find the connectedness needed to overcome feelings of aloneness and abandonment through the emotional literacy processes outlined below. These types of experiential learning processes enliven the learning environment (Beard & Wilson 2006).

Body-based holistic classroom interventions for transforming aloneness into connectedness

Group exercise 1:
the mandala of connectedness

Mandalas are a wonderful artistic form for containing learning and creating connectedness. Jung (1959) discovered their use in eastern psychology and brought them back to the west as the archetypal form for creating connectedness within the human psyche and without. Essentially, a mandala is a circular form that creates a healing and integrating space for the psyche (Watts 2002). Mandalas can be used for many purposes. You may have the child represent their life story in a mandala and the child can create as many segments as are required. One example is the use of a mandala to move from the sense of aloneness and abandonment to connectedness. Core to this mandala form is the connectedness between dimensions relating to the mineral, plant, animal, and human/spiritual realms of human experience (Cunningham 2002). This mandala is constructed by using four quadrants, one to represent each of the four primary kingdoms of human experience and is documented in Sherwood (2006) as part of the sustainable educational processes.

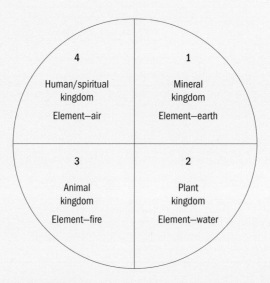

Figure 6.1 The four quadrants of the mandala

The children collect images using a collage format, or paint or draw images depending on the student's preferences that represent images that connect them to each kingdom. When they evoke these images they feel stronger, more alive, more present to the world and themselves. Children may complete these images very quickly or take some time to find them. The resource file developed in Chapter 5, is very helpful if the child becomes stuck or unable to think of an image. When this mandala process is used frequently with children, the child develops a greater capacity to deal with crises and challenges in daily life. It is through connectedness to images that the child gets a sense of relationship and through this inner strength seems to be found. Tacey (2003) in his work on Australian spirituality notes the importance of young persons accessing inner strength and the experience of interconnectedness through connections to the natural environment. He goes on to demonstrate that fragmentation of connectedness to self, to others, and to the world is a recipe for depression, suicide and addiction among youth.

Group exercise 2:
creating a sand play

Sand play is loved by children universally. It is a process developed by Dora Kalff to provide a medium for children to express their emotional life. The processes work naturally through the unconscious of the child's mind to integrate the experience back into the child's life so that it is digestible emotionally. It brings together body, mind and feelings. Pearson and Nolan (1995) note that sand play is also useful for:

- the exploration and resolution of a specific crisis
- dealing with hurts or problems
- building self-esteem
- acting out the unacceptable rather than repressing it
- creating space for emotional integration
- providing a language for feelings beyond thinking
- connecting children to their world of hope.

Materials required

- The tray should be approximately 75 cm by 55 cm by 15 cm, and ideally, wooden or plastic with a blue base that can represent water. If resources are scarce use an empty peach tray lined with blue plastic on the bottom and filled with clean beach sand.
- Water spray to wet the sand
- Have shelves displaying symbols representing both positive and negative images drawn from the mineral, plant, animal and human/archetypal realms. These images or symbols are dedicated to sand play only and are not for general use in the classroom.

- Commonly used symbols are:

Mineral	volcanos, gems, crystals, rocks, mountains, waterfalls
Plant	forests, trees, roses, flowers, fruits, cactus
Animal	tigers, lions, snakes, birds, butterflies, spiders, dinosaurs, sharks, dolphins, dogs, cats, lizards, elephants, monkeys, rabbits, frogs, fish, eagles, bees, bugs, horses, sheep, giraffes
Human	children, babies, adults (male and female), soldiers, warriors, persons, old and young, fat and thin, different cultures and backgrounds, i.e. Aboriginal Australians, Asians, Africans, Native Americans etc, clowns, sad and happy persons, mothers, fathers
Archetypal	wizards, fairies, angels, Buddha, Jesus, Mary, cross, star, crescent, magic wand, baddies, goodies
Mechanical	cars, bridges, houses, buildings, castles, fences, boats, planes, containers, food, mirrors, beds.

Table 6.1

If it is a group exercise then the teacher may direct proceedings by saying something like 'Make how you are feeling at school in the sand'. Each child will need their own sand tray and symbols if it is being done as a group exercise. Generally sand play is completed in silence but the children may sing or make sounds about the sand play as they are completing it. There is no requirement for the child to talk about it, if the child chooses not to. The sand play is disassembled but never by the person who has completed it.

Group exercise 3:
finding your special resources/'treasures' in sand play

Teaching children to resource themselves lays the foundation for an important aspect of adult mental health. With many children suffering in difficult family systems, which may be beyond the counsellor to transform and may be with parents who are unwilling or too vulnerable to commit to change, the child is left to carry the burden. Resourcing can often help the child cope in an otherwise bleak environment.

Step 1   The children are asked to choose symbols that will help them solve a difficult problem in their lives and place these in the sand tray around themselves. If the children want to they could make some special symbols for themselves from the clay and add these to the sand tray with the other pre-made symbols.

Step 2   The children name the power each symbol gives them and breathe in the power and walk around in the gesture of the powerful symbol so they can feel it in their bodily shape.

Step 3   Get the children to draw these symbols as well in their special resource folder so that they remember what symbols they find helpful in difficult emotional times.

Step 4   Remind the children that they can link to the good feeling of these symbols at any time when they need them through their thoughts and feelings.

Group exercise 4:
creating a motherhood sand play

Materials

When this is done as a group each child will require a sand tray and about 2 kg of clay.

All children at some time or other feel that they do not get enough of the positive qualities of their mother either because she is too busy, sick, unaware of their needs, has younger children or is unable to meet their emotional needs. This is a very helpful resourcing exercise to enable children to recognise the importance of maternal qualities in their lives and to celebrate mothers (it is great done just before Mother's Day). However, this exercise goes further and teaches children how to give themselves these qualities of motherhood if their mother is unavailable so that they do not have to feel totally abandoned or empty when their mother is unavailable to meet all their emotional needs. This self-parenting sequence is critical for children to learn young as part of emotional literacy and self-care. If all children acquired this skill it would also radically improve adult relationships because most adult persons project their unmet needs from their mother or father unconsciously onto their spouse and then become angry because the spouse or partner does not meet them.

Step 1

- Begin by having the children become aware of how they often feel alone or sad when their mum is busy and cannot be with them or is sick or unavailable to support them emotionally. Have the class share examples of how they feel when this happens.
- Then have the children list all the good qualities that they get from mothers. A sample selection of such qualities may include nurturing, loving, enfolding, caring, softness, tenderness, warmth, joy, fun, yummy food, encouragement.
- As a group work with one of the qualities on the list at a time as indicated in Step 2.

Step 2

For each quality named complete the following steps:

- Stand up in the gesture of the particular quality.
- Make a sound for the particular quality while you walk around.
- Breathe in the quality.
- Imagine giving the quality to yourself.
- Make the shape of the quality in clay.
- Place it in the sand tray.

When all the qualities are completed and placed in the sand tray, get them to make one big clay figure of themselves. Then after they have received all the qualities of motherhood, place the figure themselves in the sand tray.

Have a group celebration of mothers by taking photographs of these pieces and making cards for their mothers.

Group exercise 5:
creating a fatherhood sand play

Materials

When this exercise is completed as a group each child will require their own sand tray and about 2 kg of clay.

Today with the rising number of work-preoccupied fathers and single parent families, most children generally feel that they do not get enough of the positive qualities of their father either because he is too busy, absent, sick, unaware or unable to meet their emotional needs. This is a very helpful resourcing exercise to enable children to recognise the importance of paternal qualities in their lives and to celebrate fatherhood (it is great done just before Father's Day). However, this exercise goes further and teaches children how to give themselves some of these qualities of fatherhood if their father is unavailable. This way they do not have to feel totally abandoned or empty when their father is unavailable to meet all their emotional needs. This is not to suggest that this sequence is the ideal emotional substitute for the presence of a loving supportive father but it does help to fill the black holes caused by the absent father and every resource that helps the child to handle difficulties and hardships, rather than feel powerless and totally abandoned by life is to be valued as part of emotional literacy education.

Begin with a group discussion with the children about stories of missing their dad and the feelings they have when they miss their dad. Then as a group have the children brainstorm all the qualities that fathers give children that they enjoy. Make a long list of these qualities which should include strength, courage, understanding, energy, justice, protection, fun, love, knowledge, skills, and the like.

Step 1

For each quality listed undertake the following so that the quality is really experienced in the body. Ask the children to:

- Stand up in the gesture of the particular quality.
- Make a sound for the particular quality while they walk around the room.
- Visualise a colour for that quality.
- Breathe in the quality.
- Imagine giving the quality to themselves.
- Make the quality in clay.
- Place the quality in the sand tray.

Step 2

- When all the fatherhood qualities have been made in clay then sense into them all.
- Stand in a gesture that represents the totality of these fatherhood qualities.
- After having received all of these qualities of fatherhood make one large clay piece that represents themself and place this in the middle of the sand tray.

Step 3

- Have a group celebration of fathers by taking photographs of these pieces and making cards for their fathers.

Group exercise 6:
generic resourcing sequence for feelings of aloneness, abandonment and emptiness

This generic resourcing sequence is particularly effective for feelings of aloneness and abandonment. Initially the whole class works on learning this sequence together but at any time that a child feels alone or empty or abandoned they may do this sequence in the resourcing corner of the room.

Step 1

- Ask the child to identify which part of the body feels most empty, sad or lonely.

Step 2

- Ask the child to name what is missing from this part of their body in terms of qualities, that is, joy, love, warmth, fun. The child writes down a list of all these missing qualities.

Step 3

- Ask the child to choose the missing quality they need most.
- Ask the child to choose someone from their resource folder who has lots of this quality or some other person or animal that they know who has this quality in abundance.
- Ask them to imagine receiving this quality from that person.
- Suggest that the child breathe in that quality into the part of the body that is empty or sad.
- Have the child choose a colour for that quality and breathe in that colour and wrap a scarf that colour around themselves.
- Have the child walk in the bodily gesture of the new quality so the child can feel how their body is a different shape to when they feel empty and alone.

- Have the child make a sound to accompany the new gesture.
- Draw the new found quality.

Step 4

- Repeat these steps for each quality identified by the child.
- Ask the child upon completion to draw themselves full of all of these good qualities.
- Brainstorm with the child ways to reorganise their life to increase their contact with these qualities, for example, ask mum or dad for a pet, join a sport club, etc.

Individual exercises:
telling our stories to overcome aloneness—the sand play corner

All of the above exercises can be done by individual children when they feel the need to do so or at the teacher's suggestion. It is excellent when children begin to self identify their unmet emotional needs and initiate their own processes. This sand play becomes the fourth corner of the classroom which we identified in Chapter 2 as the sand play corner. Here the child is free to self-direct what they will complete in the sand play. It gives the child a splendid opportunity to make visible some inner emotional happening so that it may become digestible. Sand play enables the child to explore their feelings or to work to resolve some challenge or crisis in their life. Children from two to 12 years will spontaneously use sand play to express themselves and with great energy and enthusiasm in most cases. It gives a non-verbal language of great power to facilitate the child's emotional literacy. Weinrib (1983 cited in Pearson & Nolan 1995) identifies the power of sand play to provide the space for the recovery and expression of the emotional life.

A basic postulate of sand play therapy is that deep in the unconscious there is an autonomous tendency given the proper conditions for the psyche to heal itself. The teacher simply encourages this process by providing the dedicated space in the classroom where the inner feeling life of the child is honoured and respected.

Case study

Belinda loved sand play and was very self-absorbed and self-directed in her sand play. She initially presented as not wanting to go to school and feeling angry and frustrated when she went to school. Her sand play showed that she had few friends and she was cut off emotionally from her parents as well, often placing herself in the far corner of the tray alone with a fence between her and the other children. She placed a big fat spider between her and the other side of the fence. Over several sessions, I noted that Belinda explored different ways of placing herself in the sand play and with encouragement bringing in more and more different symbols or resources to keep her company so that she did not feel so alone. Then one day she replaced the spider with a big wizard-like figure who she said would look after her. Eventually after several sand plays of this nature, Belinda told me that she had a new friend at school. Over the period of the sand plays Belinda moved the symbol of herself from the edge towards the centre of the sand play, always a sign of increasing integration within self.

Conclusion

These exercises are not magic, and they do not pretend to be a substitute for the fully present mother or father or to completely fill the voids of aloneness and abandonment in the lives of many children today. However, they expand the child's emotional literacy vocabulary and tools to deal with life's emotional bumps and black holes. Emotional literacy should give children messages that when challenges to your heart happen in life, even though you may not be able to solve them, you can do something to help get yourself through. It is about creating an emotional consciousness of awareness and personal empowerment, rather than a victim consciousness of helplessness and hope-lessness which is a recipe for psychological collapse, pathologising labels and drug-induced dependencies. The cost, individually and socially, of failing to educate for emotional literacy in our schools is already too high.

References

Beard, C & Wilson, J 2006, *Experiential learning: A handbook for facilitators, educators and trainers*, Kogan Page, London.

Cunningham, B 2002, *Mandala: Journey to the centre*, Dorling-Kindersley, London.

Goleman, D 1996, *Emotional intelligence: Why it can matter more than IQ*, Bantam Books, New York.

Jung, CG 1959, *The archetypes and the collective unconscious*, trans. RFC Hull, vol. 9, Part 1 of *The collected works of CG Jung*, Routledge and Kegan Paul, London.

Keller, H 2003, *Optimism*, Kessinger Publishing, Whitefish, MT.

Lievegoed, B 1997, *Phases of childhood: Growing in body, soul and spirit*, Anthroposophic Press, Hudson, NY.

Pearson, M & Nolan, P 1995, *Emotional release for children: Repairing the past, preparing the future*, ACER Press, Melbourne.

Sherwood, P 2006, 'Mandalas: symbols for creating the consciousness of sustainability in Education', Proceedings of the AAEE conference, Bunbury, October 3–6.

Tacey, D 2003, *The spirituality revolution: The emergence of contemporary spirituality*, Harper Collins, Sydney.

Watts, L 2002, *Mandalas: spiritual circles for harmony*, Hermes House, London.

Don't be reckless with other people's hearts, don't put up with those who are reckless with yours.

Mary Schmich (1997)

CHAPTER 7

Bullying: freeing the victim

Big Bob was slow moving and slow thinking but a big kind-hearted fellow. He was 12 years old and loved most of all to do nothing. Big Bob came to counselling because he had been bullied by a bunch of his classmates who had followed him after school on his way home and taunted him about his weight. They had taken his school bag and thrown it into the lake so Big Bob knew he would be in trouble with his dad when he reached home. Big Bob did not like school much anyway and this was the last straw. He hated maths, reading, writing and spelling and sport and flatly refused to go back to school after the incident. He did not want to come to counselling either because he felt the situation was hopeless.

Apparently, a group of boys had been taunting Big Bob for some months ridiculing his lack of ability in sport and class work and trashing his possessions. Big Bob told me that if this was what school was about it wasn't worth doing. I liked Big Bob, because he had a kindly soft disposition and I knew he wouldn't hurt a fly. In fact, Bob was so gentle that he was the obvious doormat for more robust outgoing types of character. Bob would give up his space, give up himself, and not speak up at the slightest hint of confrontation. He reminded me of my beautiful big golden male labrador, Sam, who just wanted to be patted and accepted and loved and would never fight another dog or snarl at a person, even under provocation. I remember a black female kelpie dog that came to visit one day. She had a nasty temperament and snapped and snarled at Sam as soon as she walked onto his veranda. Although it was Sam's home territory and he was twice as big as her, rather than confront her, he would make a wide circular detour around her just for the sake of peace, every time he needed to get to his water. Sam's body said it all, 'I won't fight' and the black kelpie knew it was her way all the way to the highway. Sam's body was like Big Bob's body which said 'I won't stand up for my space, I won't fight; it is all yours'. And his class peers who bullied him knew there was no fight in him, not even for himself.

Big Bob and I talked about what would make the difference for him that would make him to want to go back to school: I insisted he tell me how he would like it to be different rather than just, 'I want the bullies to stop it'. I told him that if he changed, the bullies' behaviour would change. At first Big Bob thought I was joking but I told him of many cases of kids like him who became bully-free by developing boundaries and taking back their power. Big Bob wanted me to teach him how he could protect himself. He did not want to bash the other kids, because he did not have a mean bone in his body. We made a deal: He would come to counselling and I would teach him special ways of keeping bullies out of his space that did not require him to give a single physical punch. I explained to Big Bob about the non-verbal body languages and, over a period of five sessions, taught him a range of non-verbal tools so he could change his bodily space and energy from collapsed and giving up to strong and defensible. Big Bob was impressed.

We practised 'd.d.d's till they came out of our ears and eyes, so that energetically his one-metre boundary around himself became firm and strong. In every session we learned a new skill from the curriculum of the emotional literacy of self-defence. After three weeks Big Bob confidently went back to school. He was amazed that when he applied his new non-verbal emotional literacy tools, the bullies walked past him and left him alone. Big Bob had the same heart, but his body language was different and his use of boundary sounds was powerful. Big Bob did not return to therapy, but when I saw him by chance in the street a few months later, I could see by his walk that he had a new confidence and a new gleam in his eyes.

Bullying in schools: why current models are often failing

Despite heroic efforts by many teachers, current models are failing to effectively and consistently free the victim from being the target of children's bullying behaviours. There is too much emphasis on punishing the bully, introducing more school rules, increasing teacher patrols of the playground and, in severe cases, suspending or excluding the bully from school. Here the primary focus is upon creating safety for the victim by targeting the bully. This is the approach advocated by Rogers (2007). It is a get tough and tougher on bullies, weed them out and ensure there are dire consequences. Commendable in the short term, because it ensures safety for the victim, but a poor long-term strategy both for the victim and the bully. Who will be there to protect the victim from the bully when they are in the workforce, in intimate relationships, in sports?

Insufficient attention is devoted to supporting the victim so they can take responsibility to protect their own space in an effective way in the school system. Is the victim taught skills at school to step out of the victim role, skills to protect personal space from invasion? This is a critical aspect of emotional literacy. A number of strategies to empower the victim have been developed that employ cognitive verbal skills such as the very commendable conflict mediation processes and the speaking up strategies advocated in *The Compassionate Classroom* (Hart & Hodson 2004). In addition, Rigby (1996) notes the success of whole school approaches where children throughout the school are verbally taught the characteristics of a bully and how to speak up when they are bullied. While these are a good beginning, real sustainable empowerment for the victim must come by changing the victim's bodily languages from defeat to self-defence. The victim needs to learn the languages of emotional literacy , the non-verbal languages of sensing, sounding and gesturing which transform the victim's bodily messages from, 'I am available for abuse, I will not fight back' to 'I am not available for abuse. You will not enter my space. I will defend my space'. Only then can the victim fully and powerfully relinquish the victim role and move to the empowered speaking-up position which is not aggressive but profoundly assertive, not just in words but in the very vibrations and gestures of the body, heart and mind.

Bullies live by sensing the non-verbal language of the body. They read well the languages of fear and 'no fight in dog'. While chairing the regional child protection panel, I became aware of a survey done of child abuse perpetrators who were still bullies in manhood. Convicted perpetrators were taken one at a time to a local school playground and asked to point out the children that they would choose to perpetrate against. Not surprisingly they chose the same children, without any awareness of what other perpetrators were choosing. Then when asked why those children, the responses were also similar: 'They have body language that says they will not put up a fight, they will give up easily'. Given the increasing risk of children to adult bully perpetrators, it is urgent that we start educating children to identify victim non-verbal body language and eliminate it in themselves. Then we shall begin to free the victims from the victim body languages and their associated social role.

Body-based holistic model of emotional literacy: why it succeeds

Body-based holistic counselling identifies that, generally speaking, the bully and the victim are energetically two sides of the velcro: one has the hooks and one has the receptors and together they attract each other in an enmeshed way. In terms of balance between the head, heart and body the bullies tend to the over incarnated profile, illustrated in Chapter 2, where the bodily energies are overly concentrated in the lower pole. The lower pole energy centres govern physical survival issues, which is creativity and personal power in their positive manifestations. However, on the shadow side of these are greed, cruelty and misuse of personal power which are the core characteristics of bullying behaviour, whether in children or in adults. Such persons are prone to exploit others for their own benefit, particularly if their heart does not develop good empathy skills. The development of this will be discussed at length in Chapter 8 on freeing the bully.

In contrast, victims are prone to the developmental pattern also illustrated in Chapter 2, where the upper pole is overdeveloped and they are under-incarnated and not really present in their bodies. Often victims tend to be quiet, shy, withdrawn, day-dreamy and more interested in the world of imagination. Such children can often be very sensitive and find it difficult to hold their own in the world, and in the face of the strength of other people's threatening presence. They generally give up their space by leaving their bodies, which makes them even more vulnerable to being bullied. The victims find it easier to withdraw from this world than to stand their ground and defend their space energetically and through their body. The victim becomes freed from this position when they can learn to stay in their bodies. However, they will not do this until they learn emotional literacy skills to protect their hearts from what they experience as assaults from the world.

It is clear that we must all commit ourselves to work towards the balanced human being whose upper and lower poles are evenly balanced so that our thinking and our bodily willing can be mediated by our feeling life. Emotional literacy teaches the non-verbal skills to assist us to cultivate this balanced development and rectify our imbalances.

Emotional literacy to free the victim

The six exercises below are worth teaching to all children as part of their emotional literacy fluency although children prone to being victim will need to use these skills a great deal more often and must practise them more often. It needs to be noted that occasionally, children who are bullies may be victims, particularly if the parent is a bully perpetrator. In contrast, children that may be generally victims at school may come home and occasionally bully a younger sibling. Bullying should be regarded as a behaviour not as a personal fixed identity.

Group exercises

Group exercise 1:
occupying your own bodily space—the seven directions

Begin by explaining to the children that personal space is at least one arm's length all around their bodies. This is the space they need to fill up with themselves if they are to hold their own ground against bully behaviours. The first exercise is very simple and very empowering for children and adults alike. It is very good to keep bullies out of a child's personal space. Children prone to becoming victims need to do this exercise every day prior to walking past or confronting the bully. It is in fact a very good early morning exercise for all children to ground them in their bodies and clearly create their personal space.

Step 1   Ask children to sense how they are feeling when they stand upright.

Step 2   Ask the children to stand upright and repeat out loud their own name as they make the following gestures, for example, repeat:

Joan above (both hands stretched out above her head)

Joan below (both hands stretched out towards her feet)

Joan to the front (both hands stretched in front of her body)

Joan to the back (both hands stretched out behind her body)

Joan to the sides (one hand stretched out on each side of her body)

And Joan within (both hands to the heart while stamping the feet in unison).

Step 3   Repeat all of the above at least three times. Each child repeats their name as they do these gestures.

Step 4   At the end of the exercise ask the children to sense themselves again. Do they feel the same, stronger or weaker after this exercise? Discuss the differences they feel in their body before and after completing the exercise.

Group exercise 2:
invoking fierce compassion resources

Step 1: choose an archetype of fierce compassion

It is essential that children prone to victim behaviour acquire an archetype of fierce compassion which they can invoke by imagining that this archetype is with them in moments of threat by bullies, so they do not have to stand alone to face the potential bully. This increases the child's capacity to defend their personal space in the face of the potential bully. They should invoke this archetype to protect them even when thinking about the child who acts as a bully, and always in the presence of the child with the bullying behaviour.

This archetype is a figure that the child can see as a powerful assistant in defending their personal space. We are not talking about aggressive archetypes, but rather powerful defenders of justice and personal space. For older primary school children, Gandhi, Nelson Mandela and Martin Luther King are inspiring examples they could choose. For younger children, the archetypes may be wizards, good fairies, powerful animals like lions, and for some children they may be cartoon characters like Superman, Spiderman or Zena. They may be religious figures for some children such as St George, St Michael, the Buddha or Jesus.

Step 2   It is important that the archetype of fierce compassion chosen by the child does not remain in their head but becomes part of their bodily experience. They need to say the name of the archetype out loud, walk in the gesture of the archetype, while repeating the name out loud, until the presence of the archetype of protection is experienced in their bodily gesture.

Step 3   Have the children work in pairs to help each other find the gesture and sound of their respective archetypes and help each other practise their archetype's gesture and sound.

Step 4   Discuss with children how to use this archetype when the potential bully is around them.

The teacher may enlarge the ways of expressing the archetypal protective gesture widening the range of sensory possibilities. Beard and Wilson (2006) tabulate a multitude of sensory possibilities.

Group exercise 3:
sensing your personal space

This exercise aims to develop children's emotional fluency in understanding their personal space, which is the first step in understanding what an individual needs to protect them from the potential bully.

Step 1   Line up the class into two rows facing each other about two metres
          apart.

Step 2   Ask the children in Row 1 to close their eyes.

Step 3   Ask the children in Row 2 to walk slowly towards their partner in the
          opposite row.

Step 4   Ask the children in Row 1 to say stop when they can feel their partner
          is touching their personal space. Their partner must stop when they
          say so.

Step 5   Everyone opens their eyes and looks at their personal space and
          discusses why they need to have a boundary around it.

Step 6   Swap rows and repeat Steps 1 to 5.

Here children become aware that their personal space starts before the person
actually touches their body. In fact somewhere between one metre and half a metre,
they will notice that their partner is in their personal space.

Group exercise 4:
understanding and creating effective boundaries

This is an exercise using sound to help children understand how boundaries work.
Tagar (1996) first identified the connection between experience and certain sound
patterns. Explain to children that every person gives out a sound pattern or
vibration. Some sound patterns protect you from other people walking into your
space and some do not. The aim of this exercise is to see which sound and gesture
patterns protect you from other children walking into your space and which do not.

Step 1   Divide the children into two rows facing each other about two metres
          apart.

Step 2   One row of children makes the sound OOOO or any vowel sound. The
          other group of children walk slowly towards them and are instructed to
          stop when they sense the sound is stopping them. The children will

find that the vowel sound does not stop them and they will keep walking up to the person's face.

Step 3   Have the children gesture all the vowel sounds and suggest why they do not act as boundaries, that is, because they are open.

Step 4   Repeat Steps 1–3 but this time using the consonant 't' or 's'.

Step 5   Repeat Steps 1–3 but this time using one of the earth consonants such as 'b', 'd', or 'g'.

Step 6   Have the children identify the vowel or consonant that is most powerful in blocking entry into their personal space. Most children will identify 'd'. Occasionally a child might identify 'g' or 'b'. Allow the child to choose whichever sound makes them feel more powerful. The earth sounds are 'g', 'b', and 'd' and these are blocking sounds which are very effective in creating boundaries.

Step 7   Have all the children create a dome of protection around all directions of their personal space by speaking 'd. d. d' out loud and simultaneously with their hands gesturing the blocking gesture of 'd'. Suggest the children simultaneously imagine they are building a dome around themselves from the ground to above their heads and that they are protected by this dome.

Group exercise 5:
removing energetic invasions from your bodily space

This exercise is necessary to remove the bully energy from the victim's body. It is used when the victim has failed to protect their boundaries, to cleanse themselves of the bully energy and to re-establish their boundaries.

Step 1   Ask the children to place their hands on the part of the body where they feel the bullying energy or mean words from someone have got into their personal space.

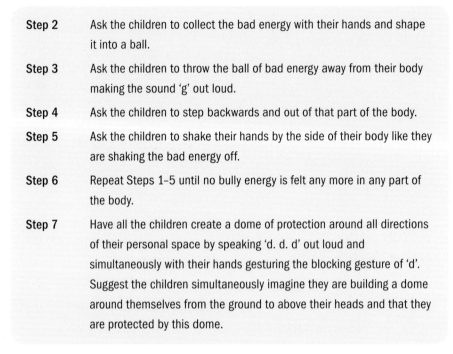

Step 2   Ask the children to collect the bad energy with their hands and shape it into a ball.

Step 3   Ask the children to throw the ball of bad energy away from their body making the sound 'g' out loud.

Step 4   Ask the children to step backwards and out of that part of the body.

Step 5   Ask the children to shake their hands by the side of their body like they are shaking the bad energy off.

Step 6   Repeat Steps 1–5 until no bully energy is felt any more in any part of the body.

Step 7   Have all the children create a dome of protection around all directions of their personal space by speaking 'd. d. d' out loud and simultaneously with their hands gesturing the blocking gesture of 'd'. Suggest the children simultaneously imagine they are building a dome around themselves from the ground to above their heads and that they are protected by this dome.

Group exercise 6:
removing betrayal energy

Often children will feel betrayed by bully behaviour especially if someone whom they regard as a friend joins the bullies. This exercise is to learn specifically how to remove the betraying bully energy from the child's personal space and how they can protect themselves from it.

Step 1   Ask the children to place their hands on the part of the body where they feel the betraying energy has entered into their personal space and sense whether they feel it is like a dagger in the back, a knife in the heart or something else.

Step 2   Ask the children to pull out the betraying energy with their hands making sounds from closed to open, that is, 'nnn' to 'arrh', as they gesture pulling out the dagger or the knife or untwisting the knot.

Step 3   Ask the children to throw the bad energy away from them and burn it up with a fire sound like 'ssshh' so that it disappears.

Step 4   Repeat Steps 1-3 until no betraying energy is felt any more in any part of the body.

Step 5   As outlined in Exercise 4, step 7, create a dome of protection around all directions of their personal space by speaking 'd. d. d' out loud and simultaneously with their hands gesturing the blocking gesture of 'd'. Suggest the children simultaneously imagine they are building a dome around themselves from the ground to above their heads and that they are protected by this dome.

Group exercise 7:
breathing the rainbow into your personal space

This exercise helps protect potential victims from potential bullies by strengthening their personal boundaries when they are about to encounter a potential bully.

Step 1   As a class exercise ask the children to imagine they are breathing a rainbow full of energy into every part of their bodies until their body is full of rainbow energy and it floods out through their fingertips and toes and fills up their personal space until there is not one crack left empty. Have them gesture the movement of the rainbow energy through their bodies as they are breathing.

Step 2   Ask the children to then choose one colour of the rainbow to create a protective dome around their rainbow space while they are saying 'd. d. d' out loud.

Individual skills

All of the above exercises are important for victims of bully behaviours because their single greatest task is to establish boundaries and stay in their bodies.

Exercises 1, 2 and 7 are the most effective for protecting themselves when walking near the bully. In the face of the bully approaching repeating 'd.d.d.d' under their breath or in their head is the single most effective gesture they need to remember. An individual prone to be a victim of bullying behaviours needs to repeat 'd. d. d' out loud while creating a 'd. d' dome every day for at least two minutes until they have developed the capacity to protect their space. The 'd' must always be crisp, like the sound of a tennis ball hitting the wall not weak and collapsed. This is very important if the exercise is to be effective (Tagar 1996). With some victims throwing or hitting a ball against a wall and repeating 'd' each time it hits the wall is essential coaching when learning to create a crisp 'd' that will hold their personal boundary.

Exercise 5 and/or 6 above are required when the bully's energy has entered the personal space of the victim as these exercises clear it out and re-establish the person's boundaries.

Conclusion

It is essential we create emotional literacy around the dynamics of the making of a victim and the dynamics of freeing the child from the victim role. To do this it is important that the non-verbal languages of emotional literacy, particularly sound and gesture, are understood by children as being effective tools that can be used to maintain and protect their personal space from the bully energy. This emotional fluency gives children the option not to be victims of potential bullying behaviours. The consequences for their adult life are considerable because if the victim role is unaddressed in the school, it continues to disempower the person in adulthood where they will become susceptible to abusive and exploitative personal and work relationships. Let there be freedom for victims from bullying behaviours and let it start with emotional literacy tools learned in the primary school classroom.

References

Beard, C & Wilson, JP 2006, *Experiential learning: A best practice book for educators and trainers*, 2nd edn, Kogan Page, London.

Hart, S & Hodson, VK 2004, *The compassionate classroom: Relationship based teaching and learning*, PuddleDancer Press, Encintas, CA.

Rigby, K 1996, *Bullying in schools and what to do about it*, ACER Press, Melbourne.

Rogers, B 2007, *Behaviour management: A whole school approach*, Paul Chapman Publishing, London.

Schmich, M 1997, 'Advice, like youth, probably just wasted on the young', *Chicago Tribune*, 1 June.

Tagar, Y 1996, *Philophonetics: Love of sounds*, Persephone College, Melbourne.

*Children need love, especially when
they do not deserve it.*

Harold Hulbert (Zubko 1996)

CHAPTER 8

Bullying: walking the bully through the doorway to empathy

Geno was a 14-year-old migrant from a deprived socio-economic background attending a regional Australian high school in an English-as-a-second language program. He was referred to counselling from the high school where he had been mainstreamed, despite the fact that his performance in reading and writing tests was equivalent to a nine-year-old's. The presenting issue was Geno's guilt and shame, the result of bullying a girl when he was eight years old. Geno had become preoccupied with his guilt to such a degree that he was unable to complete routine school learning tasks. Ironically, Geno had been bullied and was very miserable. The culprits had been reprimanded and the bullying stopped. However, while the principal was explaining to the students why they were not to bully Geno, Geno himself had had insights into his behaviour at eight years of age, when he had bullied one little girl in his class mercilessly. Now, he understood how unhappy being bullied made him, he understood how unhappy it must have made her, and he experienced strong feelings of guilt and shame which were interfering with his learning at school. He had become obsessively preoccupied with his guilt over bullying this eight-year-old girl and was unable to complete school tasks. Geno's wish was to 'stop feeling guilty and forgive himself for bullying the girl'.

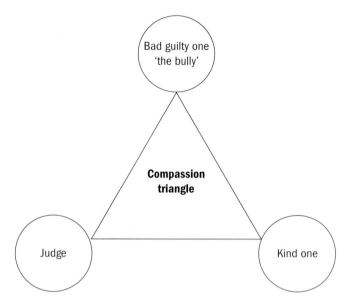

Figure 8.1 Compassion triangle

Geno's wish was to be free of the guilt and shame about being a bully and feel okay about himself again. I used a compassion triangle illustrated above. It was first developed by Tagar (1996).

Three cushions were placed on the ground in the shape of a triangle. At the right-hand angle was written the word 'kind' and a picture was drawn of two hands holding, representing the compassion position. At the apex was drawn the words the 'bad/sad one' and a picture of a tear to represent the position of the condemned one. The left-hand angle of the triangle was used to represent the judge position and the word 'judge' was written there with a drawing of a big pointing finger towards the sad/bad one. Geno helped me design these drawings and positions, so I knew that he understood the meaning of these positions.

We were now ready to start the compassion sequence so we could restore Geno's sense of inner peace. I began by drawing a picture of a human body and showed Geno that when I thought about the little girl being bullied I felt bad in my stomach and proceeded to colour in the part representing my stomach with red. I then gave Geno a piece of paper which had the outline of a human body and asked him to colour in where he felt bad when he thought about the little girl. He chose black and coloured in around his heart. We placed the drawing on the cushion representing the bad one. He told me the story again of why he was bad for bullying the eight-year-old. I then had him step into the position of the judge voice and enlarge all the reasons why he thought he was bad. He told me very simply 'I hurt that girl and she did nothing to deserve it'. I asked him to turn around and see who agreed with him and he told me the school principal and the kids in his class at school. We then found the shape of the force of the words of judgement that were cutting up his heart. He experienced them as little knives stuck in his heart. I had him pull these little knives out using a sound and gesture to accompany the task of pulling out the knives. We then proceeded to the position of the kind one who understood that he was only a little boy when he bullied the girl and did not really understand how hard it was for her. I spoke first in the position of the kind voice to the sad/bad one and then I asked him to speak in his kind voice. I asked him to turn around and see who agreed and he said that he could see his mother and his father. When I asked him if the kind one could pick up and hug the bad one and forgive him he said, 'yes'. He stepped forward to pick up the cushion representing the sad one and started to cry. He cried for nearly five minutes but it was a cry of relief as he interspersed it by saying, 'He's not really bad at all. He just didn't understand'.

There was a sense of awe in the room and I felt great reverence towards this young man, who had come back to rescue his eight-year-old from the pit of condemnation. I was profoundly moved by the goodness of this young man, as he worked to find his way back to grace. He stood there holding the cushion, which represented the previously bad one, beaming with a smile that could fill a high-rise tower. In that instant, there was an energetic transformation. The tatty clothes, the shoes falling apart, all disappeared and he became in that moment an archetype for the finest quality of the human spirit, the capacity to truly forgive self with insight and compassion, for on this foundation is built the capacity to forgive others and the capacity for empathy. I saw in that precious and profound endeavour to heal himself how cheap all the qualities of intellect and wealth are, without the riches of a human heart committed to healing itself. And the words of this young man at the moment of his realisation as he held the condemned one: 'He's not really bad at all. He just didn't understand' opened his heart to self-forgiveness. He went back to school and settled into his studies feeling peaceful and content. Geno had bequeathed the gift of faith in the potential of a human being committed to their healing, the gift of hope in the healing potential of those who become fluent with the languages of emotional literacy and the gift of witnessing the journey back to empathy with another human being (Sherwood 2007).

What is bully behaviour?

Bully behaviour can be defined as any act, physical, verbal, or emotional that intimidates or manipulates another person or invades their personal space using fear or force either overt or covert. Bully behaviour is not just restricted to children but is endemic in our society and is manifest in a number of social arenas including schools, families, intimate relationships, political and economic circles and in wars. Bully behaviours can vary in severity from taunting, teasing or belittling another human being to outrageous acts of cruelty, violence, torture and death. The current furore over bullying in schools is caused by the escalating level of violence and abuse in the continuum of possible bullying scenarios. High schools have become the arena of bullying reaching torture and death scenarios. Primary schools are also having to face sexual abuse by one child to another being perpetrated by children as young as five years of age, and violent abuse of escalating proportions. Schools are in fact a microcosm of society. We should all be radically motivated to address the bullying issues at a societal and school level as the suffering that can be created is intolerable for a society claiming to be civilised.

Why is there a bullying epidemic?

The epidemic of bullying within and outside of schools is the result of a culture that has lost contact with its heart and has failed to acquire the language of emotional literacy. The languages of the heart have been largely denied and repressed and we live numbed emotional lives in a world of consumerism and virtual reality. When the emotions can no longer be repressed and we break down or break out emotionally, the drug industry is at hand to maintain the numbness. There is a drug for anger, for grief, for anxiety, for social fears and so on. Bullying is camouflage for feelings of self-hatred, anger, revenge, low self-esteem and fear.

When the human being's heart, the centre of our feeling life, is cut off then either the lower pole which governs the willing life runs the show and is capable of cruel and sadistic acts, or the upper pole which governs thinking becomes sterile, heartless, and exploitative. The willing and thinking dimensions of a human being are capable of great and noble deeds and thoughts only when they are mediated by the heart and the feeling life. Ethics and morality come from 'the good heart' and they frame our thoughts and actions into empathetic, compassionate and respectful behaviours. When we live out of the flowing connectedness between our mind, heart and body, then we relate to other human beings from this place of connectedness and can manifest empathy which is the heart of compassion. The Dalai Lama XIV (1996), in the John Main seminar for 1995, encapsulates the meeting place of all human ethical systems as 'The Good Heart' that 'shares the common goal of producing a human being who is a fully realised, spiritually mature, a good and warm hearted person'. Regardless of the nature of an individual's spiritual commitment, or whether an individual holds a secular humanistic world view, it is generally agreed upon that a good and warm hearted person promotes peace and good will in their own lives and in the lives of those they meet. We must cultivate a new literacy of the heart life if we are to manage our feeling life to fulfil the best of our potential as human beings.

Types of child bullies in the school system

There are four main types of children that bully in the school system. These are the:

1 arrested empathy bully
2 narcissistic bully
3 abused bully
4 media-modelled bully

Different approaches are also required to address these types of bullies.

1   Arrested empathy bully

Empathy is not an innate emotional skill for all children. The critical developmental phase for acquiring empathy is between four and six years old. The young toddler is naturally very egocentric but during the period of four to six years children start to acquire empathy or the capacity to enter into another person's feelings. One of the effective processes for supporting the young child to develop empathy is for the parent or teacher to provide clear structures as to what is acceptable and respectful behaviour to other children and adults, and when the child fails to behave respectfully to have consequences which include a way back to grace. So for example, if the rules are we do not hit other children that we are playing with, then when Fred hits Tom because he wants the tractor Tom is playing with, Fred has time out with a supportive loving adult who not only explains the rule to Fred in a quiet but firm way but shows empathy for Fred's needs and teaches a way back to social grace. They might say, 'I know you really want to play with that special tractor of Tom's but it is not okay to hit him to get it. You need to go to Tom and say I am sorry for hitting you but I would really like to play with your tractor. When could I have a turn?' Through repeated processes like this Fred will learn empathy. However, if Fred has no one to provide this loving structure, either because his parents are absent or overly punitive, then Fred is likely to demonstrate empathy arrested bully behaviours towards other children with increasing intensity. Hastings et al (2000) note that empathy declines from six upwards in children with behaviour problems rather than increases as it should with age, so it becomes important to address the needs of a child demonstrating behavioural issues in a manner that helps the child return to their own heart. Otherwise a child begins to run wild with their own unmet needs for loving others and self-acceptance, and other children suffer. In adolescence, the child becomes labelled as uncontrollable or a delinquent and may be expelled from school. Bandura and Walters (1963 cited in Petersen 1989) found a significant relationship between teenage boys' delinquency and mothers' laissez faire disciplinary methods which allowed their sons to do as they pleased as children. This is particularly likely if Fred has an overdeveloped lower pole which tends to produce deeds without sensitivity to others' feelings. The empathy arrested child may have emotionally absent parents as a result of divorces, work stressors, mental illnesses or depression. These children desperately need structures to reconnect them to their feeling lives and when this consistency is provided they can overcome their bully behaviours.

Jon was a classic example of the arrested empathy type bully behaviour. His mother was a sole parent and he did whatever he wanted most of the time. He was rude to her in public and did not take heed of any of her instructions. He was in trouble from day one at preschool because he treated the teachers with the same dismissing style as he treated his mother. Jon's bully behaviour rapidly declined when it became clear that he had to conform to classroom etiquettes and structure and a suitable predictable process was set in place for Jon by the teacher. Jon also needed to be taken through exercises to create empathy and to learn to understand another person's point of view. However, it was important that his mother also undertook to complete an effective parenting training course and as a result was able to put some boundaries in place in her relationship with him.

2 Narcissistic bully

These bullies have failed to acquire empathy in the four- to six-year phase and in addition do not grow out of the egocentric phase. They become preoccupied with I, Myself and Me and have an inability to see things from another person's viewpoint. There is something very intentional about their bullying behaviours which is not evidenced in the empathy arrested bully alone who is more likely to act out of momentary frustration. Their behaviours towards other children are not so spontaneous as the arrested empathy bully. Rather they have a calculated element and they will often plan in advance to exploit, or abuse another child. The classic narcissistic bully acts as though other children are inferior and to be exploited as it suits them, and that anyone they feel is superior, namely a teacher is to be attacked. If nothing is done in primary school to challenge these behaviours and to consistently work to create empathy, these children go into adolescence with the potential to be very exploitative in human relationships. A classic example of the narcissistic bully was Rowan who was seven years old and confided in me that he plans the week ahead, targeting a different child each day to bully. He stated that each day he plans which child he will bully because he likes to feel powerful. However, when I asked him where he felt that in his body, he stepped into his heart and told me it had two sides. One side was warm and the other side was cold. He told me he could only bully when his heart was cold. When he wished to bully he would first have to freeze the warm side of his heart so it was all cold. He had a special monster that lived inside him and helped him freeze up his heart when he was preparing to bully another child.

3 Abused bully

These children are growing up in households where they are violently abused either physically, sexually, emotionally or verbally and they are living in survival mode. The slightest hint of energetic resemblance between the presenting issue in school and the family abuse experience may trigger them into anger or rage. These children are in survival mode and they often kick down the food chain. They do to their peers what is done to them by the adult perpetrators. Hence it is possible to have children whose heart space is so fractured by abuse that they are devoid of feeling towards themselves and others. Life is about 'dog eat dog'. This situation is very challenging for the school system because we are telling a child not to bully when they are consistently being bullied in the home environment, often with high levels of violence and threat. Research has shown that children, particularly boys, witnessing their fathers' violence towards their mothers, have a greater likelihood of being bullies in their school systems and in their adult lives.

Rigby (cited in Biddulph 2003) notes that a few school teachers and principals are themselves bullies towards children and belittle or humiliate children in their attempts to learn. Children usually describe these teachers as 'mean'. Such an environment does not create empathy but rather a kickback reaction where some of the recipients of this bullying will bully peers in a sad attempt to regain some self-esteem or self power. Anger and fear are often just below the surface in such bullies. Peter was a case in point. He was violently abused by his father and at the slightest provocation would resort to punching and kicking other children in a manner which was out of all proportion to the incident or the exchange in which he was engaged. Although the languages of emotional literacy helped Peter defuse his anger, his home situation remained unchanged and Peter was still prone to outbursts of bullying, although much less frequently.

4 Media-modelled bully

There is now a whole new phenomenon of bullying that has emerged with the introduction of media cultivated violence, particularly electronic games, play stations and computer games where the major aim of the game is to in some way injure another human being or to kill them. These games are created for children from preschool to adolescence and there are very few with positive themes that support the good heart. Most create not only numbness to violence but model competitive violent behaviours. When a five-year-old tells me he is going to get a girl at school and tie her down and get her raped by a lot of men then throw petrol over her and set her on fire, one is witnessing the media-modelled bully speak. A five-year-old can only articulate that idea if he has seen it in the media. The media-modelling children with bully behaviours will swiftly inform me they have seen it on 24-hour pay television, the movies, or electronic games. These children are often surprised that a range of quite violent behaviours that they have seen on electronic visual media is not okay at school. Up to a decade ago, it was the norm to expect that children sent to counselling for sexually abusive behaviours towards other children at school had experienced sexual abuse first themselves. Today, an increasing proportion of such reported abuse stems back to children witnessing such sexual behaviours in the electronic media. Bandura (1973) and other social learning theorists have pointed out for decades that children learn most from modelling by the adults around them. They found that when children observe violent fights on television, they not only copy the same aggressive actions but even add variations of violence to these gestures. Biddulph (2003) emphasises the particular importance to boys, who comprise the majority of media modelled bullies, of positive male role models in their lives. Today most children are flooded with the electronic media and its menu is predominantly one of violence and exploitation of other human beings. With this diet of violent imagery and simulated violent actions with rewards for winning, children have few opportunities to develop the good heart. Most children can give me the names of a dozen figures of violence from television or other electronic media but it is difficult to elicit from most children even two images of positive support which model the good heart that they can invoke in their life in a moment of crisis. Jonathan was a case in point. By 10 years of age he was reported for having oral sex with a female peer. Jonathan was surprised and shocked that he was in trouble. When I asked Jonathan why he had done it he replied, 'That is what you do to someone you like because I have seen it on video at home'. His family home provided Jonathan with access to 24-hour pay TV in his bedroom through which he was being exposed to many inappropriate images.

The schools are being expected to clean up the costs of the socially engineered media bully and the task is in many cases insurmountable given the time children spend with the media compared with the time the school's curriculum has devoted to bullying. Plato argued for the importance of surrounding children with images that upheld the moral values of truth, goodness, beauty, kindness, compassion, and peacefulness, proposing that they would act out of the images that were given to them. The job of curbing the media created bully cannot be left to schools. It needs to start with rigorous censorship of games for children and adolescents promoting violence and injury to other human beings. Decision-makers from families to the head of state have to reconsider the content of the electronic media and the constraints upon it. However, these decision-makers are themselves refugees from an education system that has failed to address emotional literacy, and the centrality of the feeling life to individual and social wellbeing. It is not surprising that persons who create such violent and exploitative electronic media and allow it to be publicly distributed to children are simply manifesting their own dead hearts and numbed feeling life. Their ethical values have been extinguished and they are driven by the materialist greed of the lower pole and the sterile, exploitative agendas of the hardened thinking life. It will take time to redress this critical imbalance in our culture even with a will to do it. However, the great hope is the children, for if they learn to listen to their hearts and work to create an alive feeling life then, within a few decades, a new generation of leaders will emerge whose thinking life is warmed by the good heart and whose deeds express the empathy and compassion of all great leaders.

Emotional literacy: freeing the bully to walk through the doorway to empathy

As illustrated above, bullying is a complex phenomenon and the causes of bullying behaviours are widespread from the family system to the electronic media that provides much of children's pre-packaged entertainment today. The emotional literacy of bullies is very poor so a range of exercises are recommended to develop such a language. The group exercise of empathy creation can be done by everybody in the class although, clearly, they need to be done more often by the bullies. Empathy is the single most important developmental task in the early childhood years, as this is what brings us from individuals to truly social beings (Hoffman 2000).

Group exercises

Group exercise 1:
gesturing the feeling of the bully and the bullied

Gesture is an ideal language for making outwardly visible emotions and feelings that may be difficult to detect. It is especially helpful for children who are prone to commit bullying behaviours, and who are often unaware of the impacts of these behaviours on other children.

Materials
- Two working size boards usually about half a metre by half a metre or black plastic to cover work benches.
- A water spray bottle.
- An airtight bucket of standard pottery clay in one of the earth hues.
- Three good hand-sized balls of clay for each partner.

Step 1   Have the children gesture and freeze the gesture of how they feel when someone tries to bully them, whether it is one of their peers, a parent or a teacher.

Step 2   Have them make the gesture in clay and discuss how they feel when they are in this gesture.

Step 3   Ask the children to gesture when they have been a bully.

Step 4   Ask them to make the bullies gesture in clay.

Step 5   Place the two clay pieces together and ask them to make a third piece that they can place in the middle of the two pieces, and which represents the peaceful one who can hold their own personal space.

Step 6   Have them walk around the room in the gesture of the peaceful one. Suggest they breathe the energy of this one into their bodies and make a sound for this one, usually a vowel sound.

Group exercise 2:
empathy building exercise using clay

This exercise is to develop empathy and identify and separate out a child's own feelings from the feelings of another person.

Materials

- Plastic to cover work benches.
- A water spray bottle.
- An airtight bucket of standard pottery clay in one of the earth hues.
- Three good hand-sized balls of clay for each partner.

Step 1   Have children work in pairs. One child shares a story of someone that has frightened them. The other child listens. When the child has completed telling his or her story the other child must make in clay the shape of how they think the storyteller feels about what happened to them.

Step 2   The child repeats the same story again. This time the listener is instructed to make in clay how they the listener feels about the story.

Step 3   Then the storyteller identifies which of the two pieces best represents how they feel when they are telling the story. They also share why this piece best represents how they are feeling.

Step 4   Swap roles and repeat the steps above.

This exercise can be repeated with different stories. It is excellent for creating the emotional literacy skill of empathy and helping children practise empathy in a very concrete observable way.

Individual exercises for freeing the bully

On most occasions, the bully will need to do specific activities to help themself. Most of these activities can be self-managed in the relevant corner of the classroom with the exception of Exercise 5. The precise exercises chosen will vary with the presenting issue and the emotional state most dominant in the child demonstrating the bully behaviour.

Individual exercise 1:
unblocking the anger

Group exercise 2 on identifying and defusing anger on page 50 is recommended to allow the bully to develop bodily awareness of their anger and to work to defuse it. This exercise can be completed in the anger corner and self-managed by the child exhibiting the bully behaviour.

Individual exercise 2:
working with fear

Group exercise 6 on page 82 in Chapter 5 on fear would be an excellent process for the bully to complete if they discover that their anger is really driven by fear. This could be self-managed in the clay corner of the room.

Individual exercise 3:
speaking up—unblocking the block

Group exercise 3 on page 52, in Chapter 3 on anger is excellent for bullies when starting the process of uncovering the feelings they are not speaking about, and which are often driving the bully behaviour. This can also be completed by the child self-managing in the anger corner of the classroom.

Individual exercise 4:
protecting an individual's boundaries

These exercises can be selected from Chapter 7 on the victim of the bully and are only relevant if the bully is being the victim of a bully in another situation.

Individual exercise 5:
forgiving yourself and making restitution

This exercise is relevant only to bullies who feel shame or guilt. Because it is complicated, the child will need some assistance to complete it. This sequence demonstrates the power of compassion in the self-healing process and is based on Tagar's (1996) compassion triangle. It also illustrates a precise process for changing the thought patterns that maintain self-condemnation and guilt into thought patterns of self-acceptance and loving kindness. This is important because to carry guilt and shame only increases the likelihood that the bully will have low self-esteem and continue the bullying pattern to feel stronger and more powerful. To begin a compassion triangle the child needs to recall the feeling of guilt towards the person they have bullied.

The three positions in the compassion triangle

The points of the triangle represent the three experiences within the guilty child: guilty one, judge and compassionate one (Tagar 1996). A cushion or a piece of paper with the words written on them can be placed on the ground in the following way to represent the three positions.

1 The guilty one

This is the part of the child that feels bad, ashamed or guilty.

2 The judge

The second position in the compassion triangle is the part which reacts to the condemned one with judgement and blame. The judge is the voice of a significant other: a parent, sibling, teacher or other power holder in the child's world. The judge provides the initial imprint for condemnation and judgement and the child now believes this judgement to be true, that is 'I am bad'.

3 The compassionate one

The third position is the part within the child which is capable of compassion and understanding. It is the reservoir of the positive self-healing qualities. Here the client can access the qualities needed for self-healing. In this position, all the voices of adults that have shown compassionate understanding are accessible to the child. This is the voice within the child that says: 'I understand why you did that'.

Step 1   Ask the child to draw the bad feeling they have in their body when they think about their guilt. Place the drawing on the position to represent the bad one.

Step 2   Ask the child to step into the judge position and tell the bad one why they are so bad as they point towards the bad one. When the child has finished speaking ask them to turn around and name the persons they know who would agree that they are bad.

Step 3   Here the child enters into the position of the compassionate voice which can be marked by a cushion representing the apex of the triangle. The child is asked to enter into their suffering from the position of understanding and loving kindness. Ask the child to speak from the voice of understanding, which is the voice of compassion that embraces human limitations, weaknesses, exhaustion and the feeling of being overwhelmed. Sometimes the client cannot access this voice within themself because it has been extinguished, so ask them to turn around and look behind them and see who understands why they did what they did and whether they can forgive them. Here the hope is they will find a parent, a kindly teacher or some other figure who can forgive them for their deed. If they cannot find anyone, then it is essential to stop the process and go and find a compassionate figure in their life. The child needs only to find one voice, a teacher, a friend, a significant adult who understands and values them. If someone cannot be found then go to the resourcing position and facilitate a process whereby the child finds a figure from the resource folder who can understand and forgive them. This process inevitably takes the child to the position of compassion towards self and creates a space for the expression of deep feelings, particularly grief. The child then gestures and draws the feelings of this position of beauty, softness of heart and the loving embrace of compassion.

Step 4   The child can now pick up the bad one and speak to it from the compassionate position and tell it that it is forgiven. The child can then draw the one that is now forgiven and walk around the room in that gesture. They may need to carry the cushion representing the one that was guilty and give it a hug or in some way demonstrate in gesture that this one is forgiven.

Step 5   Here is the opportunity to explore how the child can make restitution to the child they have bullied. Is it about saying sorry, writing a kind letter, giving the victim a small gift, replacing something of the victim's that was destroyed or broken, or doing some kind deed for the victim? This is part of restorative justice and essential for the child to learn the new gesture of compassion.

Conclusion

Underneath every bully behaviour is a child who has been wounded, damaged, poorly parented or missed some critical developmental phase. It is essential that as teachers we restore to the child a language for exploring and expressing their feelings and the tools to process their feelings. We cannot expect perfection but we can repeatedly remind children of the way back to grace, to the recovery of the good heart. However, the issue of bullying goes far beyond the school room. It is the single most widespread manifestation of the deadened heart of western capitalist culture where profit making is paramount even at the cost of our children's mental health, where generations have little emotional literacy and 'might is right' whether it is the family unit, the state or the nation. It is essential as a culture that we restore the heart to our educational and social processes. The 21st century needs human beings whose deeds and thoughts are softened by the warmth of the good heart, and the active feeling life that gives compassion to our deeds and understanding to our thinking. Only then can we begin to cherish the lives of those we meet.

References

Bandura, A 1973, *Aggression: A social learning analysis*, Prentice-Hall, Englewood Cliffs, NJ.

Biddulph, S 2003, *Raising boys: Why boys are different – and how to help them become happy and well-balanced men*, Finch Publishing, Lane Cove, NSW.

Dalai Lama XIV 1996, *The good heart: A Buddhist perspective on the teachings of Jesus*, Wisdom Publications, Boston, MA.

Hastings, P, Zahn-Waxler, C, Robinson, J, Usher, B & Bridges, D 2000, 'The development of concern for others in children with behaviour problems', *Developmental Psychology*, vol. 36, no. 5, pp. 531–46.

Hoffman, M 2000, *Empathy and moral development: Implications for caring and justice*, Cambridge University Press, Cambridge, UK.

Petersen, C 1989, *Looking forward through the lifespan: Developmental psychology*, 2nd edn, Prentice Hall, Sydney.

Sherwood, P 2007, *Holistic counselling: A new vision for mental health*, Sophia Publications, Brunswick, WA.

Tagar, Y 1996, *Philophonetics: Love of sounds*, Persephone College, Melbourne.

Zubko, A 1996, *Treasury of spiritual wisdom: A collection of 10,000 inspirational quotations*, 3rd edn, Blue Dove Press, San Diego, CA.

*To love and be loved is to feel the sun
from both sides.*

David Viscott (Applewhite et al 2003)

CHAPTER 9

Cultivating education with heart: the teacher's life

William was 46 and suicidal when he came to counselling. On the outside he was a successful business man with companies littered across the world. He was a man who dressed with taste and class and you could tell that his suits were probably from Rome and his shoes from Florence. He was the sort of man that people noticed. He made a point of telling me he was a self-made millionaire and that he had pulled himself up the slippery pole of success by his bootstraps. He did not believe in that social security nonsense. His childhood was rough and he was the last of seven children, all boys. He remembered vividly getting bashed by his older brothers and tied up and tormented on a regular basis. His parents were too busy to notice as they eked out a living in a poor suburban corner shop that never seemed to close or make money. He was not good at school work and his brothers and parents said he was hopeless, destined to be a failure. He described his self-esteem as pitiful by 18, but he was determined to be a huge success: 'I had to prove to everybody I was worthwhile and that is how I have done it making money and lots of it'. William married in his thirties when he was wealthy and had three children to a beautiful woman. The children were now 12, 14 and 15 and all girls whom he adored. Then, he came home from a business trip overseas, a few days before his session, to a note on the kitchen table from his wife saying the marriage was over and she and the daughters had moved interstate to the mother's home state. The note went on to list his failings as a father and partner and named a recent affair that his wife had discovered. He was devastated and said he felt like 'he had been gutted', that all that was left of him was a 'shell of a man' and he may as well be dead because he felt useless and a failure. His judgement upon himself was fierce, 'if only I'd done this or not done that'. He didn't need external judges, he was the judge and jury and he condemned himself as guilty. I asked him what he needed to want to live. He replied: 'I need to feel I have some value to somebody and not because of my money but because of who I am'. I diagnosed a compassion triangle to clear the guilt and recover his value. It was a humbling session with this powerful man on his emotional knees. When we came to the judge voice it was fierce and overwhelming and there was a gallery of judges behind him chorusing his condemnation. Yes, he had affairs, he was rarely home, he was not a good father; he was bad and deserved everything that had happened. It was a gloomy afternoon and the atmosphere in the counselling room was as oppressive. Then we moved to the compassionate voice, the one who understood and who could forgive him but he could not find this voice within himself. He turned around and looked behind him and there was no one there. It was a life and death moment in his psyche. Unless someone was there who could forgive him and see his human value, where would he find the lifeline back to the will to live. At that moment I suggested he scan back throughout his whole life and try to find at least one person who believed in his value as a human being. His heart hung in the balance as he stared behind him, then a quiet still voice spoke to save this man's will to live. 'Mrs Green, my Year 3 teacher, she saw the good in me, she saw my value, she got me through my worst year of my life at home'. He was weeping at this point and so was I. We were standing on the precipice of this man's soul and a lifeline had been found. It was his teacher Mrs Green. She would never know that she had saved this man's life; that 38 years later she stood as the only beacon of light in this man's devastated heart, the only one who believed in this man and his value that he could find. She became his model for self-acceptance and self-forgiveness. First, he received these qualities from her, breathed them into his heart and through his whole body, then he made these qualities in clay, gestured the change in his body having received these qualities and made his new gesture of self-value in clay. I knew at that moment new life had come back to his gutted soul and he would live. He had a few tough months afterwards because marriage breakdowns are never easy and we did quite a few more sessions, but he later told me that the session with Mrs Green was what made the difference between wanting to live again and wanting to die. I wanted to honour Mrs Green and all the teachers in the world who have given of their hearts and seen the beauty and goodness in a child and left in the child's heart the light of self-value. It is a priceless resource for the child's whole life. When I meet the imprints of nurturing teachers standing in the hearts of adults in therapy, I celebrate the teacher as the maker of the good heart.

The teacher as the heart of the heart of the classroom

The teacher is at the heart of the heart of the classroom. It is the teacher's heart that provides the great heart space, the emotional umbrella for all the children's hearts to gather in a protected and safe environment. When this occurs the children's emotional literacy will flourish and when their hearts are flourishing their minds and their cognitive literacy will flourish, and their deeds will reflect the warmth of engaged heart energy. What an inspiring position of trust and beneficence the teacher inherits as guardian of children's hearts.

This chapter is devoted to self-care for the teacher's heart. Teachers are asked to take on more and more; to teach emotional literacy which is a language their own education largely lacked. While in-service courses can teach teacher's processes for emotional literacy, the languages of emotional literacy are best discovered within yourself, in your own experience. So in self-care the aim is to teach the teacher the languages of emotional literacy based on self-care with its associated needs for de-stressing and debriefing.

Teachers are often very altruistically motivated and care deeply and profoundly for their students. However, they must remember that the first heart that needs their care and attention is their own heart.

Self-care for the teacher: recognising the signs that it is inadequate

Lack of self-care leads to stress build-up and if neglected tends to lead to burn out which is endemic in the education, caring and health occupations. Stress that is not processed accumulates over time to produce burn out which is defined as reduced work performance resulting from emotional exhaustion, reduced personal accomplishment and feelings of de-personalisation including loss of sense of human value (Maslach & Jackson 1981). Pines, Aronson and Kafry (1981) describe it as a chronic build-up of stress from emotionally demanding situations. Tagar (1999), working holistically from a model incorporating body, mind and heart defines stress as:

> ... a state of the whole human being in which the effect of the content taken into it is not matched by the ability of the being to process this effect. Process fails content. The system gets flooded, clogged up, blocked and poisoned by its own content. Constipation, toxicity, depletion and degeneration follow.

This is an experiential model of a human being that emphasises the metabolic relationship between experiences and the human body. In this system, toxic mental and emotional states not processed accumulate like debris in the body, mind and heart, not just slowing us down physically, but dampening our capacity to think and numbing or flooding our capacity to feel. We need to recognise that just as our body can feel clogged up by waste material; our feeling life can become weighted with unprocessed emotional material.

Sherwood and Tagar (2000) surveyed nurses' experiences of workplace stress. The key themes underlying burn-out experiences were identified as feelings of victimisation, a sense of disorientation, loss of decision-making power, lack of interpersonal boundaries and disconnection between an individual's potential and individual's performance ability. In short, in stress and burn-out, we perform well below our abilities, we become less than the human being we are capable of being.

Self-care: experiences to be addressed

In the holistic body-based model we assume that all experiences leave a residue in the mind, heart and body. In fact, the body is a map of our mental and emotional experiences as evidenced by the gestures of people's bodies. The two main categories of experiences can be named yin and yang experiences (Sherwood 2007) and it is essential to understand these to provide a quick but insightful assessment of what self-care strategies are required.

Yin experiences

First, yin experiences are a result of experiences of depletion, of absence, the lack of key qualities or inner resources that we need to be a happy healthy flourishing human being. These include Maslow's (1968, 1973) basic values of belongingness, love, self-esteem as well as his higher order 'B' values of joy, connectedness, beauty, truth, goodness and the like. When these essential qualities are consistently missing within us, we instead experience an absence of love, lack of warmth, absence of care, lack of joy, lack of connectedness, feelings of abandonment, feelings of aloneness and coldness, feelings of being overwhelmed, and sometimes fear, particularly fear of inadequacy. The yin experiences are cooling on the emotional and physical system and tend to be experienced in the body as a hollowing-out feeling, particularly at the end of the day. Common antidotes to compensate for these feelings of emptiness are sugar, alcohol, mindless shopping for unnecessary consumer goods, gambling, compulsive sex, smoking, recreational drugs and other activities that enable the human being to suppress the empty, hollowed-out feelings arising from yin experiences. In the physical body, these result in cooling illnesses such as cancer, benign growths, and multiple sclerosis. Yin experiences exacerbate the tendency to feel uncertain about your purpose in life, increase the inability to grasp a meaningful vocation, and aggravate a sense of drifting through life. Literally, they undermine self confidence in an individual's abilities in the workplace and in intimate relationships. There is a feeling of teetering on the edge of a black hole and being in the grip of the yin imprints of experience.

Yang experiences

These types of experiences occur when there are active invasions of our mind, heart and body by other people's actions, deeds or words which leave us feeling toxic, powerless, agitated, angry, anxious or irritated. Yang experiences are the result of energetic invasions into a person's energy field as a result of physical, emotional, verbal or mental abuse or trauma directed either at us or occurring around us. These energetic patterns are experienced as toxicity in the body, often to the point of feeling like you want to vomit. Literally, persons become energetic garbage bins for negative and toxic energies that have entered their energetic system because their boundaries are weak, and they are vulnerable to that particular happening because of earlier experiences in their lives, which have left them vulnerable. Consequently, the person is unable to keep their energetic space clear of these outside happenings whether or not they are directed at them. These experiences are experienced as heating in the physical body and eventually become the psycho-emotional dimension behind a range of inflammatory illnesses including tonsillitis, appendicitis, and arthritis. Behind all these illnesses, the dominating emotion is usually anger or one of its babies like irritation, annoyance, frustration or resentment. Persons with many yang experiences see life as unsafe and often feel powerless to take control of their lives, feeling overwhelmed and oversensitive to external conditions. They may feel victims of circumstances beyond their control, or overly sensitive and, in the worst scenario, they feel like emotional doormats that other people can walk over.

In essence then, it is very important in self-care to note whether the feelings of being overwhelmed, tiredness and depletion arise from primarily yin or yang experiences, or both. The type of experience indicates the types of intervention required to redress the erosion into our good health and good heart.

Self-care processes to be applied

Teachers are busy people. Not only are you responsible for educating the hearts and minds, and the emotional literacy and cognitive literacy of over 25 children in most primary schools, but you are also accountable to the bureaucratic structure of the school and education department that verifies what you are doing. This together with preparing lessons leaves little time for self-care. Hence, this needs a two tiered self-care package. First, the easy-to-use, everyday 3–5 minute de-stress, debrief package that you can do at the end of each day. Just as you shower to wash off the physical dirt of the day's work, you need to use this simple pack to wash off the energetic debris of the day that has become deposited in your heart and mind. Failing to do so means a build-up of energetic grime in the heart and mind, reduced satisfaction with your job, and less ability to bring your good heart to the fore in the classroom. In the long term, emotional and mental grime ends up contaminating the physical body and providing the psycho-emotional foundation for bodily illnesses.

3–5 minute daily self-care process kit

Eliminating the yang experiences that were experienced as toxic and contaminating

Symptoms

The signs of such experiences include two or more of the following: stress, tightness in parts of your body, thoughts out of control, repeating thoughts over and over in your mind even though the incident occurred hours ago, inability to stop agitated or critical thoughts, toxic feeling in the stomach often with stress-related lack of appetite, inability to sleep because of agitated thoughts, surges of anger or resentment, feeling like you would like to smash something or hit someone, screaming at the kids, the dog or your partner which is out of proportion to the trigger incident, driving on the verge of road rage and exploding over trivial happenings.

Interventions

1 Exercise for exiting the feeling of invasion: bamboo

The single most effective two-minute intervention is the 'bamboo' developed by
Tagar cited in Sherwood (2007) which is a short cut way for exiting unpleasant
experiences and throwing away the contaminating energy. The steps are as follows:

Step 1	Place your hands on the part of the body where you feel the tension, stress. (If it is in your head repeat Steps 2–4 until it is out of your head then recheck and find what part of the torso it is located in. Repeat Steps 2–5, this time using the place in the torso.)
Step 2	Take a step forward into that part of your body and collect the stress with your hands and shape it into a ball.
Step 3	Throw the stress away from your body making the sound 'g' (gh ... gh ... gh) out loud.
Step 4	Step backwards and out of that part of the body.
Step 5	Shake off the energy by shaking your hands and arms vigorously.
Step 6	Repeat Steps 2–4 until no fear is felt any more in any part of the body.

It is very important that the 'g' is done with a clear sharp articulation so that it
bounces off a wall. The 'g' unblocks the breath that has been blocked during the
tensions of the day. The 'g' literally reverses the nnnnngg of the stopped breathing
that has occurred during the day. Repeating the 'g' is akin to taking the top off a
bottle that is over pressured, so that the liquid can flow rather than explode. As a
matter of energetic hygiene do not throw the 'g' onto some other person's back. It is
best done outdoors or if inside directly against a wall. You know you have completed
the exercise correctly when the symptoms listed above reduce or disappear. This
exercise is not recommended when you have a headache.

2 Exercise for creating basic boundaries to keep other persons' energies outside of your personal space—'d.d.d' dome

If you notice that you are regularly flooded by other people's comments, actions and
feelings, then you probably have weak boundaries and it is adversely affecting your
mental and emotional wellbeing. You need to start reinforcing your personal space.
The simplest way to do this is every day to make a dome-like boundary all the way
around you by repeating 'd. d. d' out loud until the entire boundary of your personal

space is covered while gesturing the 'd' with your outstretched hand. This will take about 60 seconds. In the presence of the trigger person repeat 'd.d.d' in your mind. After a few weeks you will notice a remarkable reduction of your feeling of being invaded by their words or presence.

3 Exercise to ground yourself and establish your presence in your body: your name dome

Step 1   Stand upright, repeat out loud your own name as you make the following gestures, for example, repeat:

Joan above (both hands stretched out above her head)

Joan below (both hands stretched out towards her feet)

Joan in the front (both hands stretched in front of her body)

Joan to the back (both hands stretched out behind her body)

Joan to the sides (one hand stretched out on each side of her body)

And Joan within (both hands to the heart while stamping the feet in unison).

Step 2   Repeat all of the above at least three times until you feel your presence within and around you strongly.

Eliminating the yin experiences that were experienced as hollowing out and emptying

Symptoms

These characteristics include feeling flat, unmotivated, listless, unenergetic, depleted, exhausted, empty, hollowed out, run down, like you cannot face another day, withdrawn from loved ones, emotionally tired, that you are alone yet wanting to avoid friends and any emotional happenings in your life. Usually you will experience at least two or more of the above characteristics.

Interventions

You need to breathe deeply into your body and place your hand on the part of your body that seems to be the focus of these feelings. With your hand on your body list the qualities that are missing, that is, if they were there, the symptoms would diminish or disappear. Then for each of the named qualities repeat the following sequence.

Exercise with the basic resourcing sequence:

- Where in the body do you experience the missing quality?
- Invoke someone spiritual or human, living or dead, animal or being who represents the missing quality and imagine receiving this missing quality from them.
- Breathe in the missing quality to that part of your body, then let the quality flow throughout your whole body.
- Colour your breath the colour of the missing quality and continue to breathe it in for five minutes.
- Stand in the new gesture of the quality and move with your body around the room in the gesture of having received this missing quality.
- Find a sound for the missing quality and make the sound out loud.
- Draw a picture in colour of the flow of the energy of the missing quality or make something in clay to represent the missing quality.
- Reflect on how you can alter your life physically, socially or personally to include activities that will bring more of this quality into your life.

Repeat this exercise daily for 7–14 days until the energy of the new quality is alive within your body (Sherwood 2007).

The longer version self-care kit

If you notice you have persistent anger, grief and loss, fear, feelings of aloneness, guilt or self-judgement then some of the sequences recommended for the children in your class would be effective for you too. Below is a table summarising processes that can be particularly helpful for adults and you can use it as a quick reference guide. After all you are probably learning emotional literacy at the same time as teaching it and that is fine, as long as you are at least one step ahead of your children and that whenever a child is in reaction whether it be anger, fear, grief, you are not in reaction at the same time but can hold the heart space of the room calmly.

Finally, there may be times when you have exhausted your energy for self-care. Remember you deserve some care from others as well. Utilise whatever complementary health services give you a boost whether it be holistic

Feeling	Process
Fear	Group exercises 2 and 4, Chapter 5
Anger	Group exercises 1 and 2, Chapter 3
Grief	Group exercises 1 and 3, Chapter 4
Aloneness	Group exercises 1 and 2, Chapter 6
Guilt	Individual exercise 1, Chapter 8
Judgement by others	Group exercises 2 and 7, Chapter 7
Blocked speaking	Group exercise 3, Chapter 3

Table 9.1

counselling, aromatherapy, flower essences, reflexology, naturopathy, homeopathy, meditation, acupuncture, just to name a few. Remember you provide the heart that embraces all the little hearts in your classroom and you deserve all the nurturing and positives that you feel energised receiving.

Conclusion

Emotional literacy provides challenges to the schooling system and to classroom teachers but it also promises great rewards. It contains the capacity to enrich and reward the classroom learning space for when children can be in touch with their feeling life, then their thinking is enlivened with the heart's softness and warmth and their doing activities are energised with kindness and care. The languages of emotional literacy are the languages of sensing, sounding, gesturing, moving, breathing and visualising and these will greatly enlarge the classroom communication spaces. Deep heartfelt needs will be able to be communicated, and acknowledged and tools will be available to work with the core human emotions of anger, grief, fear, aloneness and low self-esteem Not only will fluency in these languages provide happier more roundly developed children, but they will move into the challenges of adolescence and adulthood with an awareness of their feeling life. They will have tools to address the basic psycho-emotional experiences of being human.

At least as important is the development of an alive feeling life generated by the good heart. This informs thinking so that it may become alive, light filled and sensitive in its dance with the heart. Then thinking will infuse human deeds with a moral and ethical dimension that has roots in the compassionate nature of the good heart. Emotional literacy, if integrated into our schooling programs, promises a quiet revolution both within schools and the wider society. From heads on legs with our hearts numbed and silenced may we move forwards to a dance of head, heart and body. Then will our thinking, feeling and willing abilities become integrated and unite to cultivate the goodness of the best of our human potential. Alexander Pope very insightfully described human beings as created: 'Half to fall and half to rise'. If we can bring emotional literacy to the lives of our children, adolescents and eventually our adult population, then surely we are integrating the 'half to fall' with the 'half to rise', and laying the foundations for a humanity in which the heart is at the centre.

References

Applewhite, A, Evans, WR & Frothingham, A (eds) 2003, *And I quote: The definitive collection of quotes, sayings and jokes for the contemporary speechmaker*, revised edn, St Martin's Press, New York.

Maslach, C & Jackson, S 1981, *Maslach burnout inventory manual*, Consulting Psychologists Press, Palo Alto, CA.

Maslow, A 1968, *Towards a psychology of being*, 2nd edn, Van Nostrand Reinhold Company, New York.

Maslow, AH 1973, *The farther reaches of human nature*, Penguin, Ringwood, Vic.

Pines, A, Aronson, E & Kafry, D 1981, *Burnout: From tedium to personal growth*, Free Press, New York.

Sherwood, P 2007, *Holistic counselling: A new vision for mental health*, Sophia Publications, Brunswick, WA.

Sherwood, P & Tagar, Y 2000, 'Experience awareness tools for preventing burnout in nurses', *Australian Journal of Holistic Nursing,* vol. 7, no. 1, pp. 15–20.

Tagar, Y 1999, 'Stress management: The use of non-verbal expression in stress management', in I Gawler (ed.), *Medicine of the Mind conference proceedings,* The Gawler Foundation, Melbourne, pp. 246–66.

EMOTIONAL LITERACY WORKSHOPS

Emotional literacy workshops for schools, parents and teachers may be arranged in your location. They comprise two-day blocks of exercises, skills and assistance to transform your classroom into a self-managing learning environment, in which hearts are at the centre.

You will leave the workshop with skills to help children and adolescents identify and transform anger, grief, fear and aloneness, and change patterns of bullying and being bullied.

For further information or bookings:

sophia.college@bigpond.com

www.sophiacollege.com

Ph: 08 9726 1505

Fax: 08 9726 1717